Gospel
Sermons
for
Children

Gospel Sermons *for* Children

60 Creative and Easy-to-Use Messages

Augsburg
MINNEAPOLIS

GOSPEL SERMONS FOR CHILDREN
Gospels, Series C

Scripture quotations are from the New Revised Standard Version Bible, copyright © 1989 by the Division of Christian Education of the National Council of the Churches of Christ in the U.S.A. and used by permission.

Cover design by Cindy Cobb Olson
Text design by Craig P. Claeys

Library of Congress Cataloging-in-Publication Data

Gospel Sermons for Children
  p. cm.
  [1] Gospels, series A
  ISBN 0-8066-2780-8 (v.1)
  1. Bible. N.T. Gospels—Sermons. 2. Children's sermons. 3. Church year sermons.
4. Lutheran Church—Sermons. 5. Sermons, American. I. Augsburg Fortress (Publisher)
BS2555.4G67   1995
252'.53—dc20
                                     95-10471
                                          CIP

The paper used in this publication meets the minimum requirements of American National Standard for Information Sciences—Permanence of Paper for Printed Library Materials, ANSI Z329.48-1984.
          ∞

Manufactured in the U.S.A.
                                       AF 9-2782

01   00   99   98   97   1   2   3   4   5   6   7   8   9   10

Contents

JEANETTE B. STRANDJORD, PASTOR
CHRIST LUTHERAN CHURCH
SPRING GREEN, WISCONSIN

Preface

Gospel Sermons for Children, based on the Gospel readings for Series C, brings you sixty new children's sermons which have the goal of communicating God's great love to children in ways they can understand. This series of three books follows the popular *Augsburg Sermons for Children* which also had three volumes.

Having a children's sermon is not the only way to let children know they are included in the worship service, but it is a good way. During this special time, the stories and messages from the Gospels can be communicated to children using words and activities appropriate to their level of development. We need to remind ourselves that children are full members of the household of faith. The fact that through these sermons we pay attention to their concerns, interests, and ability to understand is an indication that we are taking our children seriously. Even though the messages use simple language and basic concepts, the heart of the gospel comes through clearly.

The Gospel texts are taken primarily from the *Revised Common Lectionary* which is used in the worship services of a number of denominations. Most of the Gospel texts for series C are from Luke but some from John are also included. For the Sundays in Pentecost, the word *Proper*, a number, and the appropriate dates appear at the top of the page. Because the Proper texts for the Sundays in Pentecost are determined by the date of Trinity Sunday, a given text may fall one Sunday earlier or later from year to year. Children's sermons for Reformation Day, All Saints' Day, and Thanksgiving are also included, using the suggested revised lectionary texts.

The introductory material for each of the sermons provides helpful information for you as leader. Following the name of the Sunday and the reference for the Gospel text, these three sections appear:

- Focus. A brief statement of the theme.
- Experience. What you and the children will be doing.
- Preparation. What needs to be done ahead of time.

Some of the children's sermons use objects or special arrangements. However, these sermons are not like the older style object lessons that asked children to make symbolic connections between an object and an abstract spiritual concept. Abstract, symbolic thinking is beyond most children's ability.

When objects or props are part of a sermon, let the children hold them or help you with them. The children will be much more interested and also learn more from their own experience than if they simply watch you. As the children hold a stop sign, peel stick-on dots off their arms (representing leprosy), stack soup cans, make a rainbow, or look for clues to find baby Jesus, they become fully involved and feel important.

As you plan to present these children's sermons, you will bring your own style and gifts to them. Your own creativity, spontaneity, and flexibility will give energy to the messages. Children usually are eager to join in such experiences, and your enthusiasm will help them want to participate.

Your primary audience will be the children who come forward, but other children who are too hesitant or shy to participate will listen and watch. Adults and youth will also be interested in what happens and may remember the main point of the children's sermon longer than other parts of the service.

Whenever you can, include open-ended questions. Asking the children, "When have you felt afraid or scared?" or "What are you afraid of?" will lead to more interesting responses than yes-no questions like "Do you ever feel afraid?". Short-answer questions don't have to be ruled out; sometimes they serve well to set the stage for what follows.

These children's sermons emphasize grace more than rules. That is not to say that there is no emphasis on how to live. That is there, but always in the context that we are already loved. As much as possible, these messages communicate how God shows grace through Jesus Christ, how God has worked through the lives of people since biblical times, and how much God loves each of the children right now.

First Sunday in Advent

The Gospel: Luke 21:25-36

Focus: The sign of the cross is a sign of God's love for us because it is a sign of Jesus.

Experience: In a guessing-game format, the children will be asked to identify some familiar signs and one unfamiliar one. After that, the children will be shown a cross, which will be explained as a good sign, the sign of Jesus and his love.

Preparation: Using posterboard or similar material, create a set of colorful signs that will be easily identifiable: No Smoking, STOP, curve in road, school crossing, stick-figure men and women, etc. Make one sign with an obscure image, such as a planetary symbol. Also, bring a cross or a picture of one.

The Sign of Jesus

(Greet the children.) Kids, today's Bible lesson from the Gospel of Luke talks about signs. So I want to play a guessing game about signs with you this morning. Signs can be very helpful in many ways. But before a sign can help us, we have to know what the sign means, don't we? I've made some signs, so let's see if you can guess what they are. Here's the first one. Who can tell me what it means? *(Begin with one of the easy signs. Recognize and affirm their answers. Continue with the easy signs, asking, or if necessary, pointing out how each sign is helpful. Then show the obscure sign.)* Who can tell me what this sign means? *(Hopefully no one!)*

This sign can't help you, can it, because you don't know what it means. You have to know what a sign means before it can help you. *(Identify the sign for them.)* OK, here is the last sign. A lot of people don't know what this sign means, so it can't help them. Do you know what it means or what it stands for? *(Show them the cross. Recognize and affirm answers. One should be "Jesus.")*

Lots of the other signs warn us about bad things that can hurt us, like poison or cigarettes or dangers in the road and street. But the cross, the sign of Jesus, is a good sign. It reminds us that Jesus loves us so much that he died on the cross to take away our sins and make us part of God's family. When we know what this sign means, we know God loves us and that we are

God's children. This sign is very helpful! So I hope you never forget what it means. Maybe you can even tell your friends what this sign means so that they can know him, too. Jesus is our best friend, and he can be theirs, too.

Let's pray and ask Jesus to help us all *(indicate entire congregation)* tell others: Dear Jesus, we are so glad that we know what the sign of your cross means. Please help us tell others who don't know, because we want them to learn about your love for them, too. Thank you for hearing our prayer today. Amen. **–C.M.C.**

Second Sunday in Advent

The Gospel: Luke 3:1-6

Focus: This children's sermon affirms the importance of each child by teaching that God knows each of their names. And it points us to Jesus, whose own name means "God saves."

Experience: The children will count the names of people as they are read from the passage. The importance of having a name, and of knowing names, will be stressed. The meaning of Jesus' name will be emphasized in closing.

Preparation: On tagboard or newprint, using large letters, write a list of the ten personal names from this passage: Emperor Tiberius, Pontius Pilate, Herod, Philip, Lysanias, Annas, Caiaphas, John, Zechariah, and Isaiah. You will need to recruit an assistant so that one of you can read the passage while the other uncovers the names after the children say them. Use cardboard strips or another piece of newsprint (move it down as the names are read) to cover the names.

The Name Game

Good morning, kids! Are your ears working well today? Good! Because I want you to listen very carefully as I read a few verses from the Bible. And I hope your mouths are working, too. Because every time you hear the name of a person in these verses, I want you to shout out that name. I mean loud, like you are yelling at them to come in for dinner! Let's practice first. When I say a name, I will pause, then you shout it out. Some of the names are different, ones we don't hear very often. *(Introduce your assistant. Affirm and encourage a good, loud response.)*

OK, now listen carefully as I read from the Bible. Shout each name loudly after I've read it. *(Begin reading slowly, pausing slightly after each personal name, maybe repeating it. For this reading, I suggest not including the names of the regions, which will probably just be confusing. As each name is read and shouted, the assistant uncovers it on the list.)*

You all did a fine job. Look at this list. There are ten names on it! Our names tell who we are. Names help other people know us. God must think names are very important, since so many of them are in the Bible. In fact, God knows every one of us by name!

Now let me ask you something. As we get close to Christmas, a lot of

15

children are thinking about somebody in a red suit who they hope will bring them presents. What is his name? *(Santa Claus.)* Yes. And at this time of year in the church we think and sing and talk a lot about another name, the name of God's Son, who was born at Christmas. What is that name? *(Jesus.)* Yes, Jesus.

Jesus is God's Son. The name Jesus means "God saves." The Bible calls Jesus our Savior. So it is very good to know Jesus' name.

Here's another good reason to know the name of God's Son. When we know Jesus' name, we can talk to him about anything at all, just like we talk to each other. And because Jesus knows your name, guess what! When you pray, Jesus knows who is talking! And when you cry, Jesus knows who is hurt! And when you laugh, Jesus knows who is having fun. So be sure to talk to Jesus every day! He'll be very glad that you know his name. Let's talk to Jesus now as we end our time together: Jesus, thank you for being with us today. Thank you for knowing and loving us all so much. Amen. **–C.M.C.**

Third Sunday in Advent

The Gospel: Luke 3:7-18

Focus: John's exhortation, "Bear fruit worthy of repentance," gives focus to this sermon. The children learn that following Jesus calls for certain qualities (fruit) to be seen in their lives.

Experience: The sermon summarizes the story of John and mentions the need for "fruit" if we are going to follow Jesus. Using the children as trees, pictures or drawings of various fruit will be hung on them. By comparing these fruit to the inner "fruit of the Spirit," the children learn what Jesus expects of us.

Preparation: Find or make large pictures of different pieces of fruit (apple, pear, banana, grapes, pineapple, peach, cherries, etc.). On the back of each one, print in large letters one of the fruit of the Spirit (see Galatians 5:22-23) or similar words, like *sharing* and *helping*. Punch a hole or two in the top and run a string through the hole(s) long enough to hang the picture over the head of the child. Try to have a picture for each child. (Alternatives would be plastic fruit, or perhaps a non-messy real fruit, which they could eat later. In either of these latter cases, make word signs separately to hang around their necks.) Keep all of the materials in a bag or box until needed.

Fruity Followers

Good morning, children! Today I want to tell you about John the Baptist. The Bible says John was a preacher who helped people get ready to follow Jesus. And just as you came up to me this morning, lots of people came up to John the Baptist when he preached good news to them. John told them that if they were serious about getting ready to follow Jesus, they had to bear fruit. Let's find out what that means.

Now, what is your favorite fruit? *(Allow several answers.)* We have lots of fruit to thank God for, don't we? I believe all of you want to get ready to follow Jesus, so I brought you some fruit. *(Hang fruit drawings, picture-side out, on each child.)* Now what if I told you that all you have to do to get ready to follow Jesus is carry fruit around your neck all the time? Do you think that's a good idea? *(Expect mixed responses.)*

You know, the more I think about it, the more I think this must not be the kind of fruit John was talking about after all. I remember that John told the

17

people to act right and treat others right if they were going to get ready to follow Jesus. Maybe that's what he meant by "fruit." In fact, turn your picture over.

Now each of you has a word that really is another kind of fruit. Let me read them. "Love, joy, peace, patience, kindness, generosity, faithfulness, gentleness, self-control *(and other words you have added.*" We all know you don't have to have fruit hanging on you to follow Jesus. But the fruit I wrote on these papers is different. They are things you can do every day. And doing those good things helps us be to like Jesus, to remember Jesus.

I have an idea. Take your fruit-word home. Then this week you can try to do what that fruit-word says. Your family can help you. And I know Jesus will help you, too, because Jesus wants you all to be his fruity followers, not with bananas and apples around your necks, but by having good qualities in the way you live. **–C.M.C.**

Fourth Sunday in Advent

DEC. 21, 1997   DEC. 24, 2000   DEC. 21, 2003

The Gospel: Luke 1:39-45

Focus: The happiness of a surprised child illustrates the joy of Elizabeth and her baby when they heard Mary's voice.

Experience: Using the format of "This Is Your Life," the children anticipate a visit from a secret person. When he or she is revealed, the reaction of the child who is being surprised is seen by them all.

Preparation: Prepare a card with personal information from the life of one child in the group, one whose parents assure you will be there this Sunday. This will obviously be most effective if the "surprise" person really is a surprise, perhaps a grandparent or other relative who usually attends another church. Contact the guest ahead of time to discuss what you will say by way of introduction, and what he or she should say. You will also need an "offstage" microphone for them to use. A chair for the selected child will also be helpful.

A Voice to Make You Happy

Hello, children! How many of you watch television? What are some of your favorite shows? *(Allow responses.)* I remember one TV show many years ago that people liked. It was called "This is Your Life." Each week a person would sit in the middle of the stage. The announcer would tell about what had happened to this person, like where they were born and what they did with their friends. Then the announcer would say something like, "And one of those friends is here today." Then the friend, who was hidden behind a curtain, would begin to talk about the person out front, sharing stories and memories, until the person out front recognized who the hidden friend was. Then the hidden person came out, and they hugged and laughed, and had a wonderful time.

Well, I think it would be nice to try it here. So I've picked *(name of child)* as our special person today because I knew *(she/he)* would be here. Now, *(name of child)*, come over here in the middle. We're going to play "*(Name of child)*, This Is Your Life." *(Begin reading from the prepared card, mentioning such items as birth date and place, parents, first hometown, etc. Then without revealing who the person is, call for the surprise guest to speak. When the child recognizes the voice, the guest comes out and sits with the child.)*

Kids, look how happy *(name of child)* is! Why is that? *(Allow responses.)*

We did this to show you how Elizabeth and her baby, John, felt when they heard the voice of Mary. Mary, who was soon going to have a baby, and that baby would be Jesus, came to visit Elizabeth. Elizabeth was going to have a baby, too, and her baby would be named John. When Mary greeted Elizabeth, baby John jumped for joy inside her womb! *(Touch your abdomen.)* The voice of Mary made baby John and his mother very happy, just like *(name of person who came)*'s voice made *(name of child)* happy today. I wish I could have surprised all of you. But maybe this week your voice can make someone else happy, with a phone call or a special visit from you! **–C.M.C.**

Nativity of Our Lord, Christmas Eve

The Gospel: Luke 2:1-20

Focus: The traditional angel ornament atop the Christmas tree will help illustrate the visit of the angels to the shepherds.

Experience: By seeing and talking about the angel ornament many families put on their Christmas trees, the children will be helped to imagine the angels who came to announce the birth of Jesus.

Preparation: You will need a Christmas angel ornament and two or three rather outlandish alternatives (egg carton, empty pop bottle, old shoe, etc.). Put them all in a box with a lid or folding flaps. If your sanctuary has a decorated tree for Advent, an angel at its top will be very fitting. Bring a small, decorated Christmas tree with you without an ornament on top.

Look Up at the Angel

Children, I'm glad you're all here. I want you to help me make a very important decision. How many of you have a Christmas tree at your house? *(Answers. If you think some may not have a tree, you can ask, "Have you seen any Christmas trees this season?")* What do people hang on a Christmas tree? *(Lights, tinsel, icicles, ornaments, bulbs, etc.)* Great! It sounds like you know a lot about Christmas trees. So here is how I need your help. My little tree is all decorated except at the very top. I have room for one more decoration. I have decided to use one of the things in this box. But I can't make up my mind, so I want you to help me. Will you do that? *(Yes.)* Good.

Here is the first ornament I could use. *(Show one of the alternatives. Allow time for their reactions.)* Or I could use this. *(Show another alternative. Repeat until only the angel is left.)* This is the last one. *(Show the angel.)* Now which one do you think I should put on top of my tree? *("The angel!" If responses vary, just say, "Thanks, but I think I'll do what the church has done with its tree.")*

Why did you pick the angel? *(Allow responses, then conclude with the following.)* One night long ago, angels filled the sky above the trees outside the town of Bethlehem. They told them that Jesus had been born. The shepherds had to look up to see the angels. So on top of our trees at Christmas, above all the lights and balls and tinsel, where we have to look up to see it, we put an angel to remind us that Christmas is really about the birth of our Lord Jesus. So thank you for helping me pick an angel for my tree. I think this is the best choice. **–C.M.C.**

Nativity of Our Lord, Christmas Day

The Gospel: Luke 2:1-20

Focus: The baby wrapped in swaddling cloths (or bands of cloth) was a sign that the angels told the truth.

Experience: By following some simple "signs" in the sanctuary, the children will re-enact the search of the shepherds and find their own "child . . . in a manger."

Preparation: You need an infant Jesus from a nativity set or a small doll and manger substitute. Hide the baby somewhere in the sanctuary in a place where the children won't see it beforehand (near the organ or choir if you use the clues as given). Then make two or three signs or clues for them to follow to find the baby during the sermon.

A Sign for You

Merry Christmas, kids! What an exciting day! It's Jesus' birthday! Our Bible story today is about the angels coming to tell the shepherds that Jesus was born in Bethlehem. The angel who spoke must have known it would be hard to believe such good news. So the angel gave the shepherds a sign, something to help them believe the angel was telling the truth. Listen very closely and see if you can hear what the sign was. *(Read Luke 2:10-12.)* OK, what was the sign? Did you hear it? *(They would find a baby, or child, in a manger.)*

That's right. Now to help you imagine what it was like for the shepherds, I want to play a little game with you. Here is my good news for you: There is a baby Jesus in our sanctuary today, one of those little ones that come with a manger scene. And this is the first sign for you, a clue to help you find him: You will find an envelope near the pulpit *(or wherever you hid the sign or clue.)* When you find it, bring it to me. *(They find it and return.)* Look what's inside it—another sign, another clue. It says, "Look in the place where the music starts." *(Somewhere near the organ or piano, they find either another clue which you have written down, or the hidden baby.)*

You found Jesus! Now you know I was telling the truth. I'm sure it would be a lot more exciting if you had found a real live baby Jesus like the shepherds. But they did what you just did. They looked for the sign, the clue, that the angel gave them. And they found Jesus! Then they told everyone about him. And that is something we can still do today—we can tell others about Jesus and how much he loves us and each one of them. **–C.M.C.**

First Sunday after Christmas

The Gospel: Luke 2:41-52

Focus: A story of a child left behind illustrates what happened to Jesus in Jerusalem and reinforces the need for obedience to parents.

Experience: The children interact with a true, personal story that shows how children can get left behind or lost from their parents. (This really was the author's experience, but the story has been written in the third person, since others will be telling it.)

Preparation: Practice the story.

You Left Me!

Hi, kids! It's good to see you all here today. How many of you came to church alone? *(Probably none, at this age.)* No. You are too young to come by yourself. But let me tell you a true story about one child who didn't come to church alone, but got left at church alone!

Once a pastor and his wife and three children went to church. It was just like every other Sunday at first. The kids went to their Sunday school classes. The mom went to hers. And the pastor went to teach his class. Then after Sunday school they all went into the main part of the church for worship. When worship was over, the older two kids said they would walk home since it was a warm, sunny afternoon and their house was not far away. Their mom and dad were talking to some church members and having a cup of coffee. The youngest child was in a Sunday school room playing at the chalk board. The two older kids walked home. And then their mom and dad drove home, too. But there were only two children at home! Their youngest child had been left behind at church. Quickly the dad drove back to church and went in. Sure enough, there was his youngest daughter. How do you think she felt? *(Upset, scared, a little angry, relieved.)* When her dad took her home, they were all very thankful that she was found so quickly and that she was all right.

Today's Bible story says that Jesus' parents had a worse time than that! The pastor in the story I just told you lived only a few minutes away from the church where his daughter was left behind. Mary and Joseph walked a whole day toward home after they left Jerusalem! The pastor found his daughter right away, but Mary and Joseph looked for Jesus for three days! How do you think they would feel? *(Responses.)* But they found Jesus in the temple, just like the pastor found his daughter in church. The Bible says that Jesus went home with Mary and Joseph "and was obedient to them" after they found him.

You see, to stay safe, it is very important for children to obey their parents. It is very easy to get lost in a grocery store or at a mall or a movie theater where lots of people are around. So when your mom or dad says, "Stay right here," or "Don't let go of my hand," please do what they say. No one wants you to get lost or left behind. We are thankful to God for giving us parents to help watch over us and love us. **–C.M.C.**

Second Sunday after Christmas

JAN. 4, 1998   JAN. 4, 2004

The Gospel: John 1: (1-9) 10-18

Focus: We can learn about a person we don't know from someone who does know him or her.

Experience: The children will be told and shown about someone they do not know (one of the sermon giver's parents, for example) to illustrate how Jesus is able to make God known to us.

Preparation: You will need some photos and personal belongings of a friend or relative whom the children have never seen and do not know. (The description below is only an example. The actual one will be based on what items you have to show.)

Meet the Mystery Person

Kids, I have a real treat for you today. Our morning Gospel reading says that no one has ever seen God but that Jesus has made God known. Jesus was able to help people begin to know God, to know what God was like, even though they had never seen God. I want to show you how you can begin to know a person you have never seen.

(Insert your own words here as you show pictures and items.) The person is my grand-dad. His name was George Granville Howard. He was tall, with a long beard, and he must have weighed 250 pounds! Look at this. This penknife belonged to my grand-dad. He really liked this and used it a lot to whittle and carve. Here is a bird he carved for me. And here is a pin that he wore to church. Now let me show you his picture. Some people say I look like him. What do you think? *(Responses.)*

Now, even though you never met my grand-dad, I am able to make him known to you by the things I tell you and show you about him. You know some things about my grand-dad that you didn't know before. And that is what Jesus did for us. Even though we have never seen God, Jesus showed us and told us about God so we can know God better. Your Sunday school teachers try to do the same thing every week. So I'm glad you are here to learn more about God today. And even though we have not seen God yet, the Bible says we will someday, when we go to heaven.

So if you go to Sunday school every week all your life, you'll know a lot about God by the time you see God in heaven! **–C.M.C.**

The Epiphany of Our Lord

The Gospel: Matthew 2:1-12

Focus: God leads us to find Jesus.

Experience: The children will pretend to go with the wise men to find Jesus, guided by a star.

Preparation: Bring a map, three wrapped gifts, the baby Jesus from a nativity set, and a star (cut out a large yellow star and glue it on a stick). Place the baby Jesus a short distance from where the children will gather so that you must walk over to him.

When a Star Was a Map

(Greet the children.) Today I have something with me that is important when we take a trip. *(Take out a map.)* What do we have here? *(Responses. A map.)* When has anyone in your family used a map? *(Used it on a trip.)* Why did someone in your family use a map? *(So they could find the way.)*

Our story today is about some wise men whose work was to study the stars. One night a very big star appeared. God was using this star to tell them that the baby Jesus had been born. They decided they must go a very long trip to see this baby.

In that time long ago there weren't good maps like this one. *(Hold up map.)* So the wise men prayed, asking God to show them the way to find baby Jesus. God made all of the stars, so God must have decided to use one of the stars to guide the wise men to find Jesus. It was like a map for them. Let's pretend. Let's go with the wise men to find Jesus!

But before we go, we need to get some gifts ready to take to baby Jesus. The wise men definitely wanted to have gifts to bring to baby Jesus. Who would like to carry these? *(Show the three gifts you brought and let three children carry them.)* Now get on your camels and let's go. *(Pretend to climb onto camels and ride them.)* It's so exciting because we're going to see baby Jesus.

The way we'll know where to go is by the star that God put in the sky. Who would like to carry the star? *(Give the yellow star on a stick to one of the children to carry. Ask this child to hold it high. Walk with the star carrier a few steps.)* Let's all follow the star. This is the way God is showing us where Jesus is.

Now we're in Jerusalem. Let's go to King Herod *(walk to one side of your area)*. He will know where the baby Jesus is. Oh, but King Herod gets jealous. He wants us to pay attention to him, not go to find baby Jesus. So let's just leave him *(walk away)*.

It's not much farther. During the afternoon we have made it over here to Bethlehem. Here we stop. *(Stop by the baby Jesus. Have the star carrier hold the star high over where baby Jesus is.)* The star stopped right over where baby Jesus is! *(Show them the baby Jesus and let them pass him around.)* How happy we are! Now, you three children with gifts can pretend you are the wise men. You will each give your gift to baby Jesus. *(Have them place their gifts by baby Jesus.)* We praise and thank God for Jesus and that God helped us find him! We thank God for giving us this wonderful star, like a good map to find the way.

In our little play, God showed us the way to Jesus with a star. God wants us to be close to Jesus all the time, daytime and nighttime. All we need to do is ask Jesus to be with us. Let's pray. Jesus, thank you for coming to earth. We know you love us and we love you, too. Please be with us every day. Amen.

–C.C.

The Baptism Of Our Lord,
First Sunday after the Epiphany

JAN. 11, 1998   JAN. 7, 2001   JAN. 11, 2004

The Gospel: Luke 3:15-17, 21-22

Focus: Baptism means being secure in God's love forever.

Experience: The children will think about what family means and what it feels like to belong to a loving family. (Have pictures of a happy family. You could use the church directory and find different children with their families. Be sure to include single-parent families.)

Preparation: Practice the story.

Baptized Means Being Part of God's Family

Today I have some pictures of you! Pictures of you with your families. Let's look *(use pictures from the church directory, or other family pictures you might have)*. Who do we have here? *(Let them name members of their families.)*

When we belong to a family, many different things hapen. There are lots of fun and happy times. Can you tell me about times when you have fun together in your family? *(They might tell about parties, picnics, or trips.)*

When we belong to a family, sometimes there is work to be done and we all have to help out. What chores do you help with at home? *(Feed the family pet or clean their bedrooms. Encourage and affirm their responses.)* That's really great that you help. It makes you feel good when you help, doesn't it? *(Yes.)* It's really wonderful to be part of a family.

Sometimes in the family we don't want to do what our parents ask us to do, though. Has that ever happened to you? *(Wanted to watch TV or play instead.)* What happened when you didn't do what you were asked to do? *(Older brother or sister got mad at me, parents scolded me or made me help.)* Our parents make us help out because they love us very much. They have to help us learn to do what's right. Even when they scold us, they love us a lot, don't they? *(Yes.)* It's really wonderful to be part of a loving family.

And sometimes there are fights in the family. Does that ever happen in your family? What happened? *(My brother took my toy or wouldn't play with me, and I cried.)* What were your feeling when you cried? *(Angry. Lonesome.)* Yes, we feel hurt and sad when something bad happens in the family. But God gives us parents to protect and guide us, and to help us learn to get along. When we have hard times, our family is there to help us. And always in the family, we are loved very much.

Do you know that when we were baptized, God made us part of his family? God is like the most loving parent you could ever imagine. God's family is very big! Everyone in our church is part of God's family. When we hurt each other, we feel bad. But God is able to help us say we're sorry and to be kind again. God's family is so special! It's really wonderful to be part of God's family.

When Jesus was baptized, God said to him, "You are my Son, the beloved; with you I am well pleased." In the same way, God made us his children when we were baptized. God loves us so much! God chose each of you to be part of his loving family. So we never need to feel lonesome, because each of us is so special to God. **–C.C.**

Second Sunday after the Epiphany

JAN. 18, 1998   JAN. 14, 2001   JAN. 18, 2004

The Gospel: John 2:1-11

Focus: We can ask Jesus for help in rough times.

Experience: The children will hear the story of Jesus helping the host of a wedding party by changing water into wine. The children will know Jesus can help them, too.

Preparation: Bring a wedding card. If possible, also bring pictures of a wedding, a dinner, and a pitcher and glasses.

We Can Talk to Jesus

(Greet the children.) What do you boys and girls know about prayer? *(Let them tell about when they pray: mealtime, bedtime, etc.)* We tell Jesus when we're happy and when we're thankful. Do you know that we can talk to Jesus when we're worried? *(Yes.)* Can any of you tell me about some time when you've been terribly worried about something and asked Jesus to help you? *(Responses.)* I have a story about someone who asked Jesus for help. Let's see what happened.

A man was planning a big wedding for his daughter *(hold up the wedding card, also a picture of a wedding if you have one)*. What is a wedding like? *(They'll have many things to tell you so be prepared to cut them off!)* When the man who was planning the wedding saw Jesus, he said, "Your mother is coming to the wedding. We'd like you to come, too. It's going to be a great party!" So Jesus went.

It *was* a great party. There was a big dinner *(show picture' of people eating at a dinner if you have one)*. Everyone was having a wonderful time. They were laughing and dancing and eating. But then someone started passing the word around that there wasn't any wine left. How embarrassing! No stores were open. There was no place to get more wine! What would they do?

Jesus' mother felt terribly sorry for the family. She knew Jesus could help. She knew what most people didn't know—that Jesus was God's Son. She knew he could do a miracle. And so she went to Jesus and told him there was a big problem—the wine was *gone!*

Jesus saw some big empty jugs—they were like big pitchers or pails—and asked the helpers to fill them with water. Then he told one of them to fill a cup and take it to the embarrassed man who was in charge of the food.

He tasted it and was so surprised because it wasn't water anymore.

It was wine! Wonderful wine! Better than any they'd had before! When the wine was served to the people (show picture of pitchers and glasses if you have them), they asked why this very, very good wine hadn't been served first.

Jesus' disciples knew that it was Jesus who had turned the water into wine. After seeing Jesus do that miracle, his disciples thought Jesus was awesome! No one else could have done such a thing! But all things are possible with God.

And that's why we can pray to Jesus, not only when we are happy and thankful, but also when we are worried. Jesus can help us, too. **–C.C.**

Third Sunday after the Epiphany

JAN. 25, 1998   JAN. 21, 2001   JAN. 25, 2004

The Gospel: Luke 4:14-21

Focus: Jesus announced that he came to heal the oppressed.

Experience: The children will see a heart broken and recall the contrast of sadness turning to happiness out of their own life experiences.

Preparation: Cut out a large red heart and cut a zigzag through it. Use double-stick tape or rubber cement to fasten the two pieces loosely on a sheet of white paper far enough apart so it's easy to see that the heart is broken. (This story is the author's experience as a little girl but it is written in third person because others will tell it.)

Jesus Mends the Brokenhearted

(Greet the children.) What do I have here this morning? *(Hold up heart with zigzag break through it. A heart.)* What's wrong with this heart? *(It's broken.)* Yes, it is broken. Can any of you tell me about a time when your heart felt like it was broken? *(Responses.)* What feelings did you have when that happened? *(Responses. Sad, wanting someone or something back.)*

Today I'm going to tell you a story about a little girl who had a broken heart. It happened when she was seven years old. Is anyone here seven? *(Some will raise their hands.)* Well, she was just your age, and her name was Sarah. She lived on a farm where they had lots of kittens. The kittens slept in the barn where it was cozy with soft beds of hay.

One beautiful summer evening some friends came to the farm to visit. The stars were shining, hundreds of them. The moon was full and bright. While the moms and dads were talking in the house, Sarah and her friends played games outside in the moonlight. Kittens were frisking about as the children played.

When the people were leaving, one car coughed and sputtered until they pushed it down the drive. Finally, it started. But do you know, it had run over one of Sarah's favorite kittens! Can anyone tell me what it feels like when one of your pets dies? *(Responses.)* Then you know just how sad Sarah felt that night.

The next morning Sarah's father was out on his tractor making hay. He always came in about ten o'clock for coffee. When he came in that morning, he took one look at Sarah. She looked so sad. So, instead of drinking his coffee, Sarah's father took her by the hand and walked into the living room, over to the big rocking chair. He gathered her up in his strong arms and rocked as they talked about her lost kitten. She cried hard while her father held her tight. She felt his love. And somehow as they rocked, her broken heart got put back together again.

That's what Jesus promises us in our Bible reading today. He says he came to heal the brokenhearted.* *(Move the two pieces of the broken heart so they now fit together again, making the heart whole.)* So when you feel sad like your heart is breaking, you can know Jesus is with you to heal your broken heart.
–C.C.

* Isaiah 61:1, some of which is quoted in Luke 4:18.

Fourth Sunday after the Epiphany

FEB. 1, 1998   JAN. 28, 2001   FEB. 1, 2004

The Gospel: Luke 4:21-30

Focus: Jesus has good news for those who feel left out.

Experience: The children will think about people who are disabled. Three of the children will volunteer to pretend they have disabilities. A role-play will show how it feels to be rejected because of disabilities. They'll learn about Jesus' care for everyone, especially those who feel left out.

Preparation: Bring a birthday-party invitation and items for three children to pretend to be disabled (perhaps a wheelchair, a sling for an arm, and an eye patch or bandages). If a child in your group is disabled, adapt the comments and be careful not to offend him or her.

When We Feel Left Out

(Greet the children.) Jesus tells us in the Bible that he has some great good news for anyone who feels left out. Each one of you is important. And you are loved.

Today we're going to pretend that we're getting ready for a birthday party. Before we begin, I'd like three children to help me. *(Adapt the following to fit the items you brought.)* Would one of you please sit in this wheelchair? Would one of you put this sling on your arm? And I need another child to wear this bandage over one eye. Thanks, children. You three stand over there.

Let's pretend there's a birthday over here. We're getting ready for a party. How many of you like birthday parties? *(Probably all will raise their hands.)* Who has a birthday coming soon? *(Several will tell you when their birthday is.)* Let's pretend I'm a child like you and it's my birthday. I have invitations to send out *(hold up the birthday invitation)* like this one and I'm going to send them to everyone here except those three over there *(point to the three)*. I've decided I don't want to invite them because they're a little different. The one in the wheelchair couldn't play the running games, the one with the eye patch couldn't see as well to hit the pinata, and the one with the sling can only use one hand. They'd have trouble with the games I've planned for the party.

The three children over there heard about my party and know that just about everyone is going except them. How do you think they are feeling?

(Responses. Angry, sad, lonely. They might feel nobody likes them. Ask the three children to add comments.)

Let's wait a minute and think about something before we finish our party story. You've all come to church today. Jesus is here. Jesus has some great news to tell everyone. Jesus says he's come to help all who feel left out to know for sure that they are loved and part of Jesus' family. Jesus says he has come to help everyone reach out to someone who feels left out.

So that means I'd better think about my party. Could you help me? *(Yes.)* Jesus wants to help us plan this birthday party. What do you think Jesus would want us to do? *(Invite the three children.)* Yes, but remember, some of the games might be hard for them to play. Wouldn't they feel left out even if they did come? What can we do? *(Responses. We could plan games that they could play, and we could help them when they have trouble.)* Yes! When we ask Jesus to help us make plans, he'll make sure we think especially of people who feel left out.

You know, boys and girls, often we don't think of doing things the way Jesus wants. Instead, we think only of ourselves. So let's pray to Jesus and ask for his help. Let's fold our hands.

Dear Jesus, help each of us to think about people who feel left out and include them in some special way today. Amen. **–C.C.**

Fifth Sunday after the Epiphany

FEB. 8, 1998   FEB. 4, 2001   FEB. 8, 2004

The Gospel: Luke 5:1-11

Focus: Jesus sees everything in our hearts and forgives our sins.

Experience: The children will experience, with Jason in our story, that we can't hide wrongs. We need to confess what we've done wrong and be forgiven in order to have peace.

Preparation: Practice telling the story.

Jason Is Forgiven

(Greet the children.) Have you ever done something bad and tried to hide, or maybe even wanted to run away from home? *(Responses. If there are none, continue.)* Today we're going to hear a story about a boy named Jason who did something his dad told him not to do. Then he wished he could hide or run away.

Jason loved to throw stones. So did his friends. They liked to go to a football field near Jason's house and throw stones high into the air, trying to hit the field lights.

One day when they were throwing stones, Jason's dad came by. He hurried out of the car. "Don't you ever throw stones at those lights again," he scolded. "Those lights are very expensive. If you break one, we'd have to pay for it." Jason felt scared as they drove home because his father really meant what he said.

Jason never threw stones at the lights again when he knew his father was home. But one day, knowing his dad was at work, Jason went to play at the ballfield. He threw a stone that went sailing higher and farther than he'd ever thrown before. Suddenly he heard a "ping!" Glass came shattering down. He never thought he could hit his target. But he had hit it! How do you think Jason felt as he ran home? *(Ashamed, scared, worried, sad that he'd disobeyed his father.)* He did feel all of those things. He wished he could run away or hide some place. He felt terrible.

At dinner, Jason's sisters were excited and told funny things that had happened that day. Everyone was happy except Jason! Jason didn't feel like eating. His mom asked if he felt sick. He lied and said, "No, I ate some stuff at my friend's house after school, so I'm not very hungry."

What do you suppose it was like for Jason when he went to bed? *(Responses. Couldn't sleep. Maybe he cried. Tried to figure out what to do.*

Thought of running away.) It was a bad night. But he didn't dare tell his parents. The next day in school, Jason couldn't think of anything else. Jason worried about facing his family at the dinner table, but he didn't want to run away from home, either. When his mom asked again if he was sick, Jason said, "Yes, I just want to go to my room." What would you have done if you were Jason? *(Responses. Tell your dad what happened.)*

That's exactly what Jason did later when his dad was working in the living room, getting the walls ready to paint. "Dad," he said, "I did something terrible. Yesterday I disobeyed you and threw stones at the lights again. I broke one." He began to cry and said, "I'm so sorry I disobeyed you and I'm ready for whatever punishment I get."

His dad jumped down off the stepladder and went over to Jason. He got down on his knees so he could look straight into his eyes. Jason noticed some tears in his dad's eyes as he said, "You did wrong. It was a bad thing you did, Jason. But I do forgive you. We'll find a way to pay for it. Maybe you can earn extra allowance money by helping paint and clean and doing some yard work. I'm not going to punish you, Jason because I think you've had enough punishment with how bad you have been feeling." His dad wrapped Jason in his big, strong arms and Jason felt so much love. He'd deserved punishment and instead he received so much love.

Jason was so relieved to be forgiven 100 percent and to know his dad loved him. He could hardly believe what happened! Now he didn't need to run away or hide. Instead he just wanted to be close to his father. He would be happy to help him.

When Jesus forgives us, he tells us, "You don't have to feel afraid anymore now." Instead of a heavy feeling in our heart, we feel open to Jesus. We feel thankful. We feel his love. We just want to be close to Jesus and help him.

–C.C.

Sixth Sunday after the Epiphany

The Gospel: Luke 6:17-26

Focus: Jesus cares about the poor.

Experience: The children will think about the homeless and how they can actually do something to help them. They will enact a street scene in a large city.

Preparation: Bring a coat, stocking cap, gloves, and a garbage can. Have a slice of bread in the bread bag it came in, and place it in the garbage can.

Blessed Are the Poor

(*Greet the children.*) Jesus said, "Blessed are you poor, for yours is the kingdom of God." That's a very important Bible verse because Jesus really cared about the poor and wants us to help those who are poor. That's why Jesus said, "Blessed are you who are poor, for yours is the kingdom of God." Let's say Jesus' words together (*repeat them*).

Today we're going to play "Let's pretend." We need a garbage can here. (*Pull it over.*) And we need all of you to help. One of you I'll need to dress up in this coat and cap. (*Help the child put them on.*) She'll need some gloves. (*Help put them on*).

Now we're all going to pretend we're in (*name nearest city they will be familiar with*). It's winter and it's very cold. This woman (*or man*) has lost her (*his*) job and can't find a new job. There's no paycheck and no money to pay for a home and no money to buy food. So where do you think this woman (*or man*) sleeps? (*Entry way of office building, in a park, under a bridge, in a big cardboard box.*) Can you imagine how cold that must be? And what do you think this person eats? (*Soup kitchen, church where they cook meals, from garbage cans, in a shelter.*) Maybe this person has found someone who will help. But maybe she (*or he*) is still very hungry.

Let's watch this hungry person walking down the street. (*Take child by hand and pretend to be walking down the street.*) When she (*or he*) comes to the garbage can, she's going to stop. Why? (*Maybe he or she might find some food someone has thrown away.*) Exactly. And sure enough, she (*or he*) did find something to eat! (*Tell the child to reach in and take the bread*). Can you imagine eating food out of a garbage can? (*The children might make faces and say, "Yuk!"*) But if you were very, very hungry and hadn't eaten for a long time, you would eat just about anything! That's what the hungry person would do, isn't it? And that's what a lot of hungry people do. One slice or crust of bread isn't much. But it will help a little. *(Put bread and bag back in garbage can and slide it away.)*

Now let's think again about the very important words of Jesus. Jesus cares very much about the poor. So Jesus said *(have them repeat them after you say them)*, "Blessed are you who are poor, for yours is the kingdom of God."

If the poor people are so important to Jesus, I think Jesus wants us to do what we can do to help the poor. How can we help? *(Responses. Bring food for food shelf, other ideas.)* Someone mentioned the food shelf. That's a great idea. We could each bring something next Sunday *(or designated day your congregation gathers food)*. That food is given to people who come hungry and have no money to buy it.

What kind of food would be good to bring? *(Spaghetti, soup, cereal, peanut butter, powdered milk, etc.)* All of those things would be wonderful.

And let us always remember to pray for those who are poor. You will make Jesus very happy doing what you can to help the poor because they are very important to Jesus and he loves them. **–C.C.**

The Gospel: Luke 6:27-38

Focus: Jesus will help us to love our enemies.

Experience: Through a puppet story, the children will feel with Jack what it's like to be wronged and want revenge. But Jesus can help us love our enemies and that is the best way.

Preparation: Make three simple puppets. Here is one way. Using brown-paper lunchbags, lay each flat with the bottom folded down as it comes in the package. The bag will be the body of each character. Cut faces out of construction paper, drawing or gluing features and hair (you could use yarn) on them. Glue the face, down to the mouth, to the bottom of the bag. Putting your hand into the sack, you can make the mouth move when the character is talking. The three characters are Jack Sack (change his name if you don't use sack puppets), Tuffy Thomas, and Grandma. You will need one or two adult or teen volunteers to hold the script and hand you puppets while you read the parts and the narration. Practice ahead of time.

Loving Our Enemies

Jesus says in our Bible lesson today, "Love your enemies, do good to those who hate you, bless those who curse you, pray for those who abuse you." When someone is mean to you, how do you feel? *(Responses. Want to hit back, say mean things back, wish something bad will happen to them.)* We all have those feelings. It's only Jesus who can help us love and be kind when someone is mean to us. We have a story about that today. So just sit back while our puppets tell their story. *(Have a volunteer hold the script as you read it. Have the three puppets lined up on a table.)*

JACK: Hi, I'm Jack Sack. *(Move the sack so it looks like he's talking.)* It's summer vacation and I'm riding my bike over to Grandma's house. My grandma is the greatest grandma in the whole world. *(Knocks on her door; you could say, "Knock, knock.")*

GRANDMA: Well, do come in, Jack. Say, there's a new boy named Tuffy who just moved in next door. Why don't you invite him to play with you?

JACK: That sounds like fun. I'll take my bike so we can ride together.

(Jack rides to Tuffy's house. He's sitting on the front step, looking grumpy.)
Hi, Tuffy, I'm Jack. Want to ride bike with me?

TUFFY: Will you let me ride yours? *(Jack lets him. They play a while and then Jack goes back to his Grandma's house.)*

GRANDMA: Well, did you find a new friend?

JACK: Tuffy is just like his name. He seems kind of mean.

GRANDMA: Maybe he's just lonely because he's new here.

The next day Jack can't find his bike. He hurries over to Grandma's house.

JACK: Grandma, my bike is gone. What could have happened to it?

GRANDMA: Maybe you should look in the park where you were playing. Sometimes we forget where we leave things.

Jack goes out searching. As he walks by Tuffy's house and sees his bike under the bushes. Tuffy comes out of the house.

JACK: Tuffy, I just found my bike under your bushes.

TUFFY: That's *my* bike and don't you take it! *(Jack goes back to Grandma.)*

JACK: Grandma, I found my bike under the bushes by Tuffy's house and he says it's his and that I'd better not take it. He's a thief and he's mean. I hope something terrible happens to him.

GRANDMA: *(Puts her arms around Jack.)* Jack, we all want to get even when people do something bad to us. But Jesus said we should love them and do something good to those who harm us. We can't love our enemies though, unless Jesus helps us. So let's ask Jesus. Please, Jesus, help Jack to find a way to be kind to Tuffy today. Amen.

JACK: Maybe Tuffy would like some cookies and milk with me!

GRANDMA: That's a great idea. *(Jack walks back down the street. Tuffy comes out.)*

JACK: Tuffy, my grandma makes the best cookies. She's the best Grandma! Would you like to have some with me?

TUFFY: Sure. *(He follows Jack. They enjoy the cookies and have so much fun talking together.)*

That night Grandma helps Jack pray. They ask Jesus to soften Tuffy's heart and make him want to bring back the bike. The next morning there is a knock on the door. It's Tuffy.

TUFFY: I didn't sleep very well last night. You were all so good to me. The cookies and everything. I felt real guilty because I stole your bike, Jack. I'm really sorry and so I brought it back.

GRANDMA: We'll forgive you, won't we, Jack? Tuffy, maybe you don't have a bike.

TUFFY: No, I don't. We don't have enough money to buy one. I sure wish I had a bike.

GRANDMA: Tuffy, I've got weeds in my garden and I need my lawn mowed each week. If you work for me, you'll soon earn enough money and we'll help you get your own bike.

TUFFY: That's great. I'll work real hard. I *do* want a bike! You *are* a good grandma!

What do you think would have happened to Tuffy if Jack had been mean to him, too? *(Responses. He might have gotten meaner.)* What helped Jack be kind? *(Grandma helped him. Jesus helped him.)* Yes, and Jesus will help us be kind to others even when they are mean. Jesus can put love in our hearts.

–C.C.

The Gospel: Luke 6:39-49

Focus: We can keep learning from Jesus and following Jesus.

Experience: Through hearing the story of the house on the rock and the house on the sand, the children will learn that their lives can be safe if they keep listening to and following Jesus.

Preparation: In a cake pan, place a flat rock, two tiny houses like those from a Monopoly game, and dampened sand the size of the rock. Place one house on the sand and the other on the rock. Bring a pitcher of water.

Build Your House on the Rock

In our Bible lesson today, Jesus has something very important to teach us about how we live our lives so we stay very safe with Jesus. Jesus says we must keep listening to him all of our lives. How can we learn about Jesus and find out what he wants us to do? Where can we listen? *(Responses. Listen to Bible stories, listen in Sunday school and church, listen to parents and grandparents. Repeat the good things the children say to affirm them).* Yes, Jesus wants us to listen in all of these ways.

But Jesus wants us to do something more than just listen. When your parents tell you to come in to eat, what do they want you to do besides listen? *(Responses. Come in right away.)* When your parents ask you to take out the garbage, what do they want you to do besides listen to them? *(Take out the garbage.)*

It's the same with Jesus. Jesus wants us not only to listen, but to do what he asks us to do. When we know Jesus loves us, we will want to do what pleases him. We feel safe knowing Jesus loves us. The Bible says that's like having our house on a good, solid, rock foundation.

Watch now what we're going to do here. *(Bring out cake pan with sand, rock, and two houses, and the pitcher of water.)* We have two houses. The houses are the same. But something is different with these two houses. What's different? Take a look at where they are. *(One is on a rock, the other is on sand.)* Yes, that's right. Let's look to see what happens to the two houses when the rains come. We'll pretend it's raining. *(Gently pour water on the house on sand).* What's happening to that house? *(It's sliding away, falling.)*

Now let's look to see what happens when it rains on the other house. *(Pour gently.)* Is this one going to slip away or fall, too? *(Keep pouring.)* It just keeps raining and raining and raining. Finally the rain stops. What happened? *(The house on the rock was safe.)*

Jesus wants us to be so sure of his love for us that we feel safe. Then we will want to listen to him. And besides listening, we'll want to do what he asks us to do. Then, we'll be like the house built on the rock. So let's listen in Sunday school and church and at home, and ask Jesus to help us do what he wants us to do. **–C.C.**

The Transfiguration of Our Lord,
Last Sunday after the Epiphany

FEB. 22, 1998   FEB. 25, 2001   FEB. 22, 2004

The Gospel: Luke 9:28-38 (37-43)

Focus: The presence of God is awesome.

Experience: The children will think about an important person they'd like to come and visit them and what the visit might be like. This will prepare them for the transfiguration story.

Preparation: Practice the story.

Someone Important Comes to Visit

If you could choose someone very important to come for a visit, who would it be? (*Responses. Grandparent, teacher, President, sport hero. Come to an agreement.*) Let's pretend you did invite (*name of person*) and this special person is coming to your house tomorrow. What feelings do you have knowing (*name*) is coming to your house tomorrow? (*Excited, can't wait.*) What would you do to get ready? (*Clean my room, buy special food, make a welcome banner, invite my friends.*) What would you like to talk with (*name*) about when this person comes? (*Responses.*)

Once, a very long time ago, Peter, James, and John, three of Jesus' disciples, had a chance to talk with a very special person. It was Jesus. Jesus had invited just the three of them to hike with him up a mountain. For once there wouldn't be crowds of people around. They could talk to Jesus and pray together. Peter and James and John were so excited! Jesus was a very important person to them. It would be so wonderful just to be with Jesus!

They hiked quite a while, and when they got to the top of the mountain, something very surprising happened. Two very important people appeared that Peter, James, and John never dreamed they'd see—Moses and Elijah! They had lived a long time ago and here they had come back! Then something else happened, they heard God's voice! They couldn't see God, but they heard God say, "Jesus is my Son, my Chosen, [so be sure to] listen to him." Being with God and with Jesus and with Moses and Elijah was the most wonderful thing that had ever happened to them.

It was fun to imagine being with the person we chose, (*name of person, review what you talked about earlier*). It is even more awesome to be with Jesus, the Son of God, our best friend. Jesus is with us all the time, at home, here in church, at Sunday school, whereever we are. It's awesome to be able to talk with Jesus and to have him as our very own friend! **–C.C.**

The Gospel: Luke 4:1-13

Focus: Jesus chose to experience the same feelings and temptations that we do in life.

Experience: The children will see that the devil offered Jesus three ways to avoid doing what God wanted, that Jesus said "no," and that he was willing to experience life.

Preparation: Find or draw four pictures: one each of 1) bread, 2) money, 3) a temple or tall building, and 4) Jesus.

Jesus Chooses You

(Greet the children.) Today we have a very good story in the Bible about Jesus. Jesus was in the desert where it was very hot and dry, and he was very hungry and tired. Can you show me with your faces and bodies how that must feel when you're hungry? Tired? *(You may lead the children by looking sad, holding your own stomach, then slumping over with eyes shut.)* Yes, those are good ways to show how it feels to be hungry and tired.

It was OK for Jesus to feel hungry and tired because one of the reasons God sent Jesus to be with us was to feel the same things we do. God sent Jesus to live like we do, so Jesus could talk to us, teach us, and help us.

Now, the devil in our Bible story wanted to stop Jesus from doing what God wanted. The devil tried three ways to make Jesus choose things that would make him different from other people, not like us.

First, the devil said, "Jesus, turn these stones into bread and you will never have to feel hungry again." *(Hold up the picture of bread.)* Then the devil said, "Jesus if you will worship me I will give you all the money and power in the world." *(Hold up a picture of money.)* The devil was saying that Jesus would never have to be tired or work again. Finally, the devil told Jesus that Jesus should use God's power to protect him from any kind of danger or from ever getting hurt. The devil told Jesus to jump off the temple *(hold up the picture of a temple or building)* and see if God would protect him.

Wow! The devil was offering Jesus a lot of things. Let's think about them. I need three helpers now to hold these pictures. *(Have each child hold one picture and stand up on one side of the group.)* Now I need one more helper to hold this picture of Jesus and stand on the other side. *(Have this child represent Jesus and stand opposite from the other three children.)*

Remember the devil was telling Jesus that he could have bread—lots of money—and never, ever get hurt if he would just listen to the devil. The devil wanted Jesus to obey him instead of God and to forget all about God's plan that Jesus love us and be one of us. The devil said Jesus would have all of these things *(point to the three children holding the pictures of bread, money, and building)* if he *(point to child holding picture of Jesus)* would forget about feeling the hunger and hurts we feel, if he would forget about us and forget about obeying God.

That was quite a choice. And do you know what Jesus chose? Jesus chose to say "no" to the devil. He chose to do what God wanted. He loved you and me that much. *(Name of child holding picture of Jesus)*, please sit down with all the children to show us that Jesus chose to be with us and to love us. We are more important to Jesus that anything else in the world.

Let's put down our pictures and then all of us can fold our hands, close our eyes and pray. Dear Jesus, thank you for choosing to do what God wanted, to be with us, and to feel what we feel. Thank you for loving us so much. Amen. **–J.B.S.**

The Gospel: Luke 13:31-35

Focus: Jesus loves and protects us the way a mother hen loves and protects her baby chicks.

Experience: Through acting out imitations of animals, the children will experience what it means to say Jesus is loving and protecting like a mother hen.

Preparation: Find a picture from a storybook or Bible storybook of a mother hen and her chicks.

Like a Mother Hen

(Greet the children.) Sometimes we use animals to help tell us what someone is like. I'll give you an example. If I say, "He is as strong as an ox," what do you think of? Let's all stand up. Now can you show me what you would look like if someone said you were as strong as an ox? *(Children can flex biceps, pretend to lift something, other responses. You may also lead by example.)* Good. Now, let's try this one: "That person is as gentle as a lamb." Can you show me what you would look like if you were as gentle as a lamb? *(Children may smile, hop around lightly, other responses.)* Let's try one more. Sometimes people say, "She's as happy as a lark." A lark is a bird what whistles and flies around. Can you show me how you would look if you were as happy as a lark? *(Children may try whistling, smiling, waving their arms, other responses. If your space doesn't permit much movement, have them stand still while "flying.")*

That was fun and you did a fine job of acting out all of those things. In the Bible we read about Jesus. Sometimes the Bible says that Jesus is like a shepherd who watches his sheep. Can you pretend to be a shepherd watching his sheep? *(Children may pretend to carry a lamb, reach down to pet a lamb, hold hand above eyes to search the distance, step in place, other responses.)*

In one of our Bible stories for today it says that Jesus is like a mother hen. I have a picture here to help us think about that *(hold up a picture or drawing)*. What is in the picture? *(Responses.)* That's right, this mother hen has lots of baby chicks. The Bible says that Jesus is like this. Jesus is like a mother hen *(point to the hen in the picture)* and we are like the baby chicks *(point to chicks)*.

Can anyone tell me what a mother hen does when something dangerous is going to happen, like a rainstorm or when some animal wants to hurt her baby chicks? *(Responses may be general such as helps them or gets mad.)* A mother hen has two big wings *(point to picture)*. When her chicks are in danger from bad weather or from someone who wants to hurt them, she raises her wings and the chicks can hide under them and be safe. Would you show me what it would look like to be a mother hen gathering her chicks? *(Children sweep the area in front of them with their arms, other actions.)* Good! Thank you. You may sit down again.

Jesus says that he is like a mother hen. He came to bring us close to him and to protect and help us. That is very good news. Jesus loves and protects us just like a mother hen loves and protects her chicks.

Let's thank Jesus for that right now. Please fold your hands and we will pray. Dear Jesus, thank you for loving and protecting us like a mother hen loves and protects her chicks. Amen. **–J.B.S.**

Third Sunday in Lent

The Gospel: Luke 13:1-9

Focus: To repent means to stop and look to Jesus.

Experience: Through the use of a sign, the children will learn that to repent involves 1) stopping and thinking about what we are doing and 2) turning to Jesus who points us in the right direction.

Preparation: Make a two-sided stop sign and mount it on a dowel or stiff strip of cardboard. On one side, make a red stop sign with the word "STOP" in bold letters. On the other side, glue or tape on a picture of Jesus.

Stop and Look to Jesus

(Greet the children. Hold up your sign so that the word "STOP" is visible to the children.) What does this sign say? *(Stop.)* If someone is driving a car, what do they do when they see a sign like this? *(Responses.)* That's right. When Mom or Dad is driving they will put the brakes on and the car stops. Then Mom or Dad look around to make sure it is safe to start up again.

I want us to think about this stop sign today because it has something to do with what Jesus is saying to us in our Bible reading for today. Jesus tells the people and us to repent. When Jesus says, "Repent," it is like saying, "Stop" *(hold up the stop sign and point to it)*. Jesus wants people to stop and look at themselves and then ask, "Am I doing what God wants me to do?

Let's practice that. Now, watch the sign and when I raise it up high like this *(raise the sign)* you all say "Stop, repent!" *(Put the sign down and then lift it up once, they say the words for practice.)* Good! Now I'm going to talk about some times when we need to stop. Listen to me and watch the sign. *(Put the sign down with the stop side up.)*

Here is something for you to think about. Pretend you are at home and are playing with a friend. Your friend breaks one of your toys. He doesn't mean to but it makes you mad and you *(raise your free hand)* are ready to hit him *(at this point raise up the stop sign and you and the children say, "Stop, repent!")*. That's right! We stop and think about whether or not we should be hitting. Friends aren't for hitting. Jesus wants us to stop before we hit. It would be better to talk about the problem and work it out. *(Put the sign down again.)*

Or suppose you are at school and another student drops her lunch tickets on the floor. Someone else picks them up and hides them in their pocket and. . . . *(at this point raise up sign and children respond, "Stop, repent!")*. Right! Jesus doesn't want us to steal things either. *(Put the sign down.)*

Jesus tells us to stop for a reason. He loves us and doesn't want us to hurt other people. He says *(raise the sign for children to respond with "Stop, repent!")* so that we will look at him *(turn sign over so the children can see the picture of Jesus)* and think about what Jesus wants us to do. *(Put the sign down.)* It is good to say, "Stop, repent!" but then always remember to look at Jesus. Jesus loves you and will help you do what is good and right.

Let's close our eyes and fold our hands and talk to Jesus about that right now. Dear Jesus, help us to stop when we think about hurting others. Help us to look at you each day. Help us to love you and other people. Amen. **–J.B.S.**

Fourth Sunday in Lent

The Gospel: Luke 15:1-3, 11b-32

Focus: God has limitless love just as the father in the parable of the lost son loves both his sons in spite of their wastefulness (younger son) and resentment (older son).

Experience: By hearing a summary of the story and using paper hearts, the children reflect on the great and generous love of God.

Preparation: Bring a globe or world map. Cut out a large, red paper heart. Cut out a number of small, red paper hearts so there are enough to give at least two to each child at the close of the sermon. You may wish to recruit an adult or older teen to help you distribute the hearts.

No Limits to God's Love

(*Greet the children.*) Who has ever said to you, "I love you no matter what happens" or "I'll never stop loving you"? (*Give time for possible responses, such as Mom, Dad, Grandma, or Grandpa. Be aware that some may never have heard those words.*)

That is a wonderful kind of love. It means that even when we are bad we are still loved. Mom or Dad might not always like what we do but they still love us very much.

Jesus tells us a story in the Bible about a dad who was like this. This dad had two sons, and both of these sons did some bad things. The younger son went away from home and wasted all his money. The older son got very angry at his younger brother and at his dad, too.

Listen to what the dad said to both his sons, even though they had been bad. He said, "I love you no matter what happens. I'll never stop loving you." That is like what I hope your parents say to you. And one thing we know, it is what *God* says to you. God, like a loving mom or dad, loves *you* no matter what happens. God doesn't always like what we do. There are times we can get angry, we hit people, or we won't share with others. God doesn't like that but God still loves us. God loves us *and* everyone else.

Let's think about that for a moment. Let's say that this heart (*hold up the large paper heart*) reminds us of God's love. Now where could I put this heart to show who God loves? (*Wait for responses or prompt with questions.*) Could I put it on me? Could I put it on (*select adult from congregation*)? How about you?

I could put this heart on everyone here, because God has enough love for each of us. I could also *(bring out the globe or map)* put this heart on people all around the world *(hold heart up to several different parts of globe or map)*. It does not matter how old they are, or what color their skin is, or whether they have made big or little mistakes. Just like the dad in Jesus' story, God loves us no matter what.

God is not selfish with love. God passes it all around to lots of people. Today I'm going to give you each some hearts *(pass out paper hearts, two per child)*. Keep one for yourself so you will remember how much God loves you, and give one to someone else today and tell them it means God loves them no matter what. *(If there are many children, have a helper come forward to distribute the hearts as children leave.)* Thank you for helping to pass God's love along to other people. **–J.B.S.**

The Gospel: John 12:1-8

Focus: Mary's gift said "thank you" to Jesus for all he had done. We can say thank you to Jesus, too.

Experience: By focusing on Mary's gift to Jesus and talking about ways to say thank you, the children will find ways to thank Jesus for his gift of love to them.

Preparation: Choose a gift you have received (such as book or article of clothing) to use as an initial example. Place a bow or ribbon on it to help the children visualize it as a gift. Have a cross (or picture of one) to hold up for the children to see.

Thank You, Jesus

(Greet the children.) I had a nice surprise the other day. I received a thank-you gift. (Hold up your gift.) I had helped someone (insert a name if you would like to) move some furniture (or another example). It was hard work but I wanted to help. I didn't expect a gift but it was a nice surprise.

Has that ever happened to you? Have you ever received a thank-you gift or a thank-you hug for helping someone? (Give children time to talk, then sum up with something like the following.) It is nice to receive gifts and thank-you gifts like these. And it is good to say thank you to people.

Our Bible story today is about saying thank you and giving a thank-you gift. A woman named Mary gave a thank-you gift to Jesus. Listen to this Bible verse that tells us about it: "Mary took a pound of costly perfume made of pure nard, anointed Jesus' feet, and wiped them with her hair" (John 12:3).

At the time Jesus lived, people wore sandals all the time and their feet got dirty a lot. So when people came to your house, you would wash their feet to be nice to them and help them. This is what Mary did for Jesus. But she did not use water. Instead, she used a very expensive perfume. It was so expensive that it would take a whole year to earn enough money to buy it. That was quite a gift!

Mary's gift was a very big thank you gift. I wonder why she was so thankful. What had Jesus done for her? Do you have any ideas? (The children may respond with general remarks such as he helped her, loved her. Nod your head and accept these.) Yes, I'm sure Jesus did all of those things for her. He even made her brother Lazarus alive after he had died. So Mary really wanted to say thank you.

Jesus does some very nice things for you and me, too. He helps us, he promises us a home in heaven after we die and he died for us *(hold up cross)*. And on Easter morning he rose for us to be with us always.

Now, I wonder how you and I can say thank you to Jesus for all these things. Any ideas? *(If responses are few, you could suggest saying thank you in our prayers. Then continue.)* Remember Jesus said he wants us to help others. That would be a good way to thank Jesus. What could we do? *(Children mention ways to help others.)* These are all good ways to say thank you.

Let's do one of them right now. Let's close our eyes, fold our hands and pray. Dear Jesus, thank you for loving us so much that you would die on the cross and then come back to us on Easter morning. Amen. **–J.B.S.**

Sunday of the Passion, Palm Sunday

The Gospel: Luke 23:1-49

Focus: Jesus met the crowd's anger and cries for crucifixion with a prayer for forgiveness. God granted his prayer.

Experience: By leading the children through the biblical description of the angry crowd, they will begin to understand Jesus' situation, and his love and forgiveness even for his enemies.

Preparation: A picture or pictures of Jesus' trial before Pilate and the mockery by the crowd would be useful in talking about this passage. Otherwise bring a picture of Jesus that has a loving expression.

God's Wonderful Forgiveness

(Greet the children.) Our Bible reading from Luke tells us about a very sad time in Jesus' life. It was a time when many people were angry and mean to Jesus. Listen to what the Bible says the people did. The people shouted, "Away with this fellow!" and "Crucify, crucify him!" * "Crucify" means to kill someone. The people were really mad at Jesus *(hold up pictures of the crowd if you were able to find some)* and wanted to kill him.

Jesus' friends did not help much either. They were so afraid of the angry crowd that they just kept quiet and didn't try to help Jesus. So Jesus was all alone. Can you show me with your faces how it would feel to be all alone like Jesus with lots of people mad at you? *(You and the children try looking sad.)* How would it feel to be angry? Remember that the crowd was angry. *(All can make angry faces, maybe raise fists.)* How would it feel to be afraid like Jesus' friends? *(Hide heads under arms, look afraid.)* *(If possible, take time with each of the three examples to ask questions like these: I think that is a sad look, am I right? Is that an angry look? An afraid look?)*

When you and I feel sad, afraid, and mad, what are some of the things we might do? *(Be open to various responses, such as cry, run away, yell, or hit. Suggest some of these if the children are shy about answering.)* I know that when people are not nice to me I have some of those feelings and I may feel like doing some of those things.

Maybe Jesus felt like doing some of those things, too. When we look at our Bible story we see what Jesus *did* do. Jesus asked God to forgive the

* Luke 23:18, 21

people. Jesus didn't yell at the people. He didn't run away. He didn't fight with the people either. No, he asked God to forgive them (hold up picture of Jesus). Jesus wanted God to help the people and give them another chance.

That's just what God did, too. God is so loving that he will help people and give them another chance. God did that for those people who were mean to Jesus and God will do that for you and me, too. Even if you and I do some wrong things, God will still try to help us and give us another chance. That is really good news.

Let's say a prayer of thanks for that right now. Dear God, thank you for loving us and giving us another chance even when we are mean and angry. Amen. **–J.B.S.**

The Gospel: John 20:1-18 or Luke 24:1-12

Focus: The children will see that God has provided many ways for things to change, including the change from death to life through the resurrection.

Experience: The children will think about four kinds of change: growing up, new life, metamorphosis, and resurrection.

Preparation: Prepare four signs, each with one of the following words on it: growing up, new life, metamorphosis, and resurrection. Add drawings, pictures, or magazine cutouts to illustrate each word in appropriate ways (some are mentioned below).

Four Kinds of Change

(Greet the children.) As you look around you can tell that today is special. What's different today? *(Responses. There are Easter lilies and flowers everywhere. We heard trumpets. People are dressed up.)* You may also have noticed that the colors in church on the pulpit and banners, and the stole the pastor is wearing *(if you are the pastor, say "I am wearing")* are white instead of purple. White is the color of Easter. Things look different because we have changed some things. We have changed things because today is Easter, a day of great change.

Let's talk about different kinds of change. Sometimes people talk about changes they see in each one of you. Has anyone ever said to you, "My, how you have grown"? *(Responses. Grandmas and grandpas, relatives.)* You are bigger. That's one kind of change, isn't it. We call that kind of change growing up. This sign says "growing up." *(Show them the sign and talk about the measuring stick or other drawings on it.)*

There is another kind of change that spring brings. What happens outside when spring comes? *(Flowers start blooming in the yards. Trees are budding. Green grass. Robins.)* Yes, certain birds have returned and the colors we see outdoors are changing to green and other colors. I'm going to call this change "new life." Here is a sign about it. *(Show the sign and point out the tulips, trees, birds, or whatever is on it.)*

Soon we will see another change. We'll start seeing butterflies. During the winter there weren't any butterflies. Do you know where butterflies come from, what they used to be? *(First they are caterpillars, then they spin cocoons around themselves .)* Scientists use a big word when they talk about this change from caterpillar to butterfly. It's "metamorphosis." It's a hard one. Can you say it with me? *(Sound it out by syllables: Met-a-mor-pho-sis.)* Very good! *(Show the sign for "metamorphosis" with pictures of caterpillars, cocoons, and butterflies.)*

Now, one more kind of change, the kind of change that Easter is all about. Jesus died on the cross on Good Friday, but on Easter morning he was alive again. We call this kind of change a "resurrection." Can you say that? *(Resurrection.)* *(Show the "resurrection" sign with a picture of Jesus.)* He was dead, then he was alive again. That's why we're so happy at Easter!

You see, boys and girls, life is always changing. Look at our four signs. They show there are many kinds of changes. The best change of all is the resurrection. Jesus lives, and after we die, we will get to live with him. Let's all say, "Amen." *(Amen.)* **–W.C.Y.**

Second Sunday of Easter

APRIL 22, 2001   APRIL 18, 2004

The Gospel: John 20:19-31
Focus: Jesus is with us when we are afraid.
Experience: The children think about being afraid, and using locks and keys. Then they will talk about how they can pray to Jesus when they are afraid.
Preparation: Bring a lock and key.

Locking Out Fear

(Greet the children.) What is this that I brought along today? *(Show them the lock you brought along. Let them pass it around. Allow responses.)* Why do we use locks on our doors and cars and bikes and other things? *(We're afraid of being robbed. To keep strangers out. To feel safe.)* We often use locks to feel safe. But what if we were coming home and wanted to get inside. What could we use to unlock the door? *(A key. Show them a key.)*

We read in the Bible that after Jesus died, and even after he was alive again, Jesus' disciples locked the doors when they were together because they were afraid. Can you imagine what they were afraid of? *(The children may not know; prompt them. The disciples were afraid of the people that hated Jesus. Maybe those people would come and hurt them.)* Yes, they were afraid bad things might happen to them. Well, they couldn't stay locked up forever just because they were afraid. Before long, Jesus came to them. They knew he had died, but there he was, alive again. How glad they were to see him! They talked together and soon felt much better. Jesus' love for them was like a key that unlocked their fears.

When we are afraid, we can talk to Jesus, too. What are some times when you have felt afraid? *(Responses. Storms, someone mad at them, having to go to the hospital. Keep the sharing brief.)* One thing we can do when we feel afraid is to talk to Jesus. What do we call it when we talk to Jesus? *(Put your hands together in a prayer position. Praying.)* Yes, praying. We can pray to Jesus, anytime we are scared. We know he loves us. When we pray to Jesus we can tell him how we feel. We remember his promises to be with us and then we will not be quite so afraid. There are times when we need to use locks on our doors or bikes or cars. But anytime we are afraid, we can talk to Jesus. We know Jesus loves us and is with us. His love for us is like a key to unlock our fears. Let's pray *(have the children fold their hands)*. Jesus, we thank you for loving us and being with us. We know we can pray to you whenever we are afraid. Amen. **–W.C.Y.**

Third Sunday of Easter

APRIL 29, 2001   APRIL 25, 2004

The Gospel: John 21:1-19
Focus: We, like the disciples, are thankful for the power of the risen Christ.
Experience: The children will first think about the two sides of their bodies and other familiar objects, then they will hear an after-Easter Bible story about Jesus and his disciples and two sides of a boat.
Preparation: Bring a Bible.

Two Sides to Everything

(Greet the children.) Girls and boys, have you ever wondered why God gave us two hands, two feet, and two of quite a few things? What do we have two of on our bodies? *(Have them touch or move the parts they name. Arms, hands, legs, feet, ears, eyes, nostrils. Stop with those.)* Why do you think God gave us two of these things? *(Responses. If we couldn't see out of one eye, we'd still have another. Two legs help us stay balanced. Other responses.)*

A lot of the time it's good to have two ears and two of other things, isn't it? Two ears means that you can hear from either side of your head, and you don't have to keep twisting your head around to hear someone. *(Demonstrate and have them move their heads.)* We can hear people from either side of us. *(Mention and point to sounds in your church that come from different places: organ, choir, readings, preaching, hymn singing.)*

Of course, if we did lose one arm or leg or eye, we could get along, and some people are born without one or the other, and they manage. How can they do that? *(Guide the responses to avoid offense. They can be fitted with a prosthesis, learn use one arm or hand in better ways, etc.)*

Just about everything has two sides, like this Bible *(show front and back)*, this church building *(point to left and right)*, our houses, your toys *(name some)*, your clothes, your bed, our cars, lots of things.

The Gospel story for today tells about a boat and its two sides. This happened after Jesus had died and became alive again. His disciples went fishing in a boat, but they didn't have a very good day. They hadn't caught one single fish! Then they saw a man standing on the beach but they didn't know it was Jesus. When Jesus heard that they hadn't caught any fish, he called to them, "Try the right side of the boat. You'll catch some fish there." Sure enough, they switched from the left side to the right side, and guess what! They caught 153 fish in their net just like that. Wow! Then the disciples knew who it was who had talked to them—it was Jesus! Once again he helped them when they were having a rough time, and again they realized how powerful he was.

So today we have reviewed how God gives us two of some things on our bodies and two sides to just about everything. How thankful we are to God for making things the way they are, but we are even more thankful that Jesus is alive and powerful and keeps on loving us and helping us every day of our lives. **–W.C.Y.**

Fourth Sunday of Easter

MAY 3, 1998   MAY 6, 2001   MAY 2, 2004

The Gospel: John 10:22-30

Focus: The children will learn about the shepherd's care for sheep and hear about Jesus' care for them.

Experience: You will play the role of Sam or Sally the shepherd and will describe some aspects of being a shepherd. You will tell them that Jesus is your good shepherd and theirs, too.

Preparation: Find or make a shepherd's staff. You could use a walking cane, although it is rather short. To make a staff, take a five-foot piece of plastic plumbing pipe and tape on a curved neck or crook cut from cardboard. For a rod, you can use a solid tree branch, maybe about three feet long. You could drive eight to ten big nails in one end (they make it more powerful as a weapon). Wear a headdress or bandana. You could also wear a tunic, sandals, and other biblical clothing if you wish. If you can find a picture of Jesus as the good shepherd, bring that along.

The Shepherd Cares for the Sheep

Hello! I am *(Sam or Sally)* the shepherd. I can't stay long, but I want to talk to you about what shepherds do. I've been climbing these hills and walking these valleys so long that I need to rest a little. Soon I have to get back to my sheep. Right now they are resting over in the shade.

I brought along a couple things to show you that I use to care for my sheep. This one is called a crook or a staff. The word *crook* sounds like crooked, doesn't it? *(Yes.)* And that's what it is; this top end is bent over, it's crooked. *(Let them feel your homemade staff or your cane if that's what you brought.)* I use it in three ways. One is to hook the sheep when they go walking off where they shouldn't go, or to pull them up if they fall. See how this crooked end can curl around their neck? *(Demonstrate by hooking your other wrist with it and pulling it toward you.)* A second use is to poke the sheep with the straight end. *(Poke the air near you.)* Some may be going too slow, so when I poke them they hurry up and catch up with the others. A third use is to lean on it when I walk. I do get tired, and it helps me keep my balance when I'm walking in rocky places. *(Demonstrate walking with it.)*

This other piece is my rod. It's kind of heavy. *(Let them feel it.)* Guess how I would use it if a wolf came after one of my sheep. *(Responses. Hit the wolf with it. Scare the wolf so it leaves.)* I don't want any wild animals to have lamb chops for dinner! *(Say more about any nails pounded into it or other characteristics that make it a stronger weapon.)*

When night comes, I take my sheep back home and put them in a pen. Do you know where I sleep? *(Responses. They may not know.)* I sleep right in the doorway of their pen. So do you think any wolves or other wild animals *(show your teeth, growl)* can get in and hurt my sheep? *(No.)* And can any of my sheep get out and run away? *(No.)* So they are very safe and they sleep well.

A shepherd's life can be dangerous. But I enjoy the work and I love my sheep. One lamb got lost yesterday and I searched and searched and finally found her. She was stuck between two rocks on a cliff. Do you know which tool I used to reach down to help her get loose? *(Responses. The staff with its crooked end. Pretend to loop it around a lamb and pull it toward you. Say something like, "Wow, am I ever glad you're all right!")* I brought her back to the other sheep and they were glad to see her, too.

The Bible tells us that Jesus is our good shepherd. He's not a shepherd of sheep, but of people, of you children, of everyone here, and of me, too. He loves us and cares for us. *(Show them a picture of Jesus as the good shepherd if you have one.)* He knows all of your names, and he loves every one of you. He doesn't want you to get lost or hurt. Jesus tells us, "Children, come to me. I love you." Let's all say to him, "Thank you, Jesus. We love you, too." *(Say this again, having them repeat the phrases after you.)*

Well, it's time for me to go back and care for my sheep. Thank you, children, for listening so well. **–W.C.Y.**

Fifth Sunday of Easter

The Gospel: John 13:31-35
Focus: We are called not to hate but to love.
Experience: The children will think about why some people hated Jesus, how everyone sometimes feels hateful, and what they can do to change those feelings and be more loving.
Preparation: Practice the story.

Love One Another

(Greet the children.) One reason we come to church is because we love Jesus. What are some of the reasons that we love Jesus? *(He loved everybody. He healed people. He forgave people. He was kind. He died for us.)* We love Jesus for the good things he did and for the kind of person he was.

Can you imagine that when Jesus walked on the earth, there actually were people who did not love him? Why do you think some people hated Jesus? *(Help the children think of reasons. They were jealous of him because he was so popular. Some people hate everybody. Some people are mean.)* Those are all good answers.

People hated Jesus for some of the same reasons that people hate each other today. They hate people for being more famous, or having more things, or looking so good, or getting their way, or winning when they didn't, or whatever. Sometimes even you and I hate people. Maybe we don't say, "I hate that person." We may say, "I don't like that person," or "That person is ugly, stupid, or weird." But underneath, it's hate.

What can we do when we start feeling that we hate somebody? One thing we can do is to pray. We can ask God to help us be more loving and forgiving. Then we can talk to other people about how we feel *(maybe our mom or dad or a friend)* and try to figure out ways to be loving instead of mean. What do you do to get over being angry or hating someone? *(Responses. Ask parents what to do, talk to the person I'm angry with, be alone for a while. Steer children away from ideas of revenge.)* Sometimes we just have to stay away from someone we hate for a while until our feelings cool down. Our feelings can change. God does help us.

Let's imagine two different days and how you would feel at bedtime. Think about how would you feel on a day when you've had some fights, you are mad at people, and maybe you even hate someone. Then think about a different day and how you'd feel when you had been loving and kind to your friends and family. Which day would feel better, the first day or the second day? *(The second day. We feel good when we've been loving and kind.)*

God knows that love is the best way. When we love each other, we feel so much better and happier than when we fight and hate each other. The Bible tells us how loving Jesus was. Do you know what Jesus did when people hated him? He loved them anyway. That's not easy to do, is it? *(No.)* Jesus said, "Just as I have loved you, you also should love one another." Loving each other may not always be easy, but it's the best way and God will help us. Each day, keep thinking about Jesus words about being loving.

Let's pray. God, help us to be loving. It isn't easy. Help us to get over being hateful. Thank you for Jesus. I know that Jesus loves me. Amen. **–W.C.Y.**

Sixth Sunday of Easter

The Gospel: John 5:1-9
Focus: The children will think about what they can do for themselves and what they need help with.
Experience: The children will think about what they could do at different ages and what they needed help with then. They will also talk about learning to ask for help when they need it now, including asking God for help in prayer.
Preparation: Bring pictures of a six-month-old baby, a two-year-old child, and a mirror.

Helping Yourself and Asking for Help

(Greet the children.) Boys and girls, let's think about the things that we can do for ourselves and the things that we need help doing. Let's think of what we can do at different ages.

Let's first think about being about six months old. *(Show the picture of a six-month-old baby.)* Do you know any babies about this big? *(Responses.)* What could you do for yourself when you were six months old? *(Cry. Drink milk. Smile. Wave hands and kick feet.)* What did you need help doing? *(Getting dressed, fed, bathed. Being put to bed. Being carried from place to place.)*

Now let's think about when you were two. *(Show picture of a two-year-old.)* What could you do for yourself when you were two years old? *(Walk around. Run around. Pick up things. Talk a little. Put things away. Eat with a spoon.)* What did you need help doing? *(Zipping up clothes. Buttoning them. Cutting out things with a scissors. Taking a bath.)* And do you remember how you got that help? *(Responses.)* Either someone like your mom or dad did it or you said, "Help me."

What about the age that you are right now? How old are you now? *(Responses. Hold up a mirror and pass it around.)* What can you do for yourself now? *(Responses will vary by age. Dress ourselves. Brush our teeth. Set the table. Get in the car. Walk to school or the school bus. Ride a bike.)* You can do almost anything, can't you? But there are still things that you cannot do. Like maybe bake a cake without help. Like maybe read some of the big words in the Bible or other books, or take care of your baby brother or sister all by yourself. And how do you get help when you need it. *(Ask for it!)*

Sometimes we are afraid to ask for help, like the man in the Bible story who sat by a pool of bubbling water for thirty-eight years hoping someone would help him get into it so he would be healed. As far as we can tell, he never asked anyone to help him!

Sometimes we might be afraid to ask for help because we think that someone will laugh at us or make fun of us. We think we should be able to do something for ourselves, but we really can't and so we don't. Sometimes we don't do things for ourselves because we're afraid that we will make a mistake and fail.

There is an old saying, "Better to have tried and failed then never to have tried at all." It's also better to ask for help and be refused than never to ask at all. Often when we ask, we do get the help we need. We can ask many people around us. Who are some people we could ask when we need help? *(Responses. Mom, Dad, Grandpa, Grandma, friends, teachers, others.)* There's someone else we can talk to and ask for help, too. Who is that? *(Put your hands in a prayer posture. Responses. God.)* Yes, God wants us to ask for help in our prayers. God's answers come in many ways, usually through people like our mom or dad or others who love us.

Let's pray. God, thank you for all the things we can do. And thank you, God, for all the help you give us with parents and friends and teachers and many other people. Amen. **–W.C.Y.**

Seventh Sunday of Easter

The Gospel: John 17:20-26
Focus: In the church we are all united in Christ, yet that unity includes much diversity.
Experience: The children choose their favorite colors, decide when those colors are appropriate and not appropriate, and then build a rainbow to illustrate the variety and unity of the church.
Preparation: Bring enough sheets of red, orange, yellow, green, blue, and purple construction paper so that each child can have a piece in his or her favorite color. Ask an assistant to help you. You might also alert some friends to help out with the extra colors at the end.

One Rainbow, Many Colors

(Greet the children.) Girls and boys, today let's think about the colors of the rainbow. I have here in my hand six of them: red, orange, yellow, green, blue, and purple. Which of these do you like the best? *(Some may name colors you don't have, like pink. Tell them to choose from what you have.)* Hold up your hand when I call the color you like, and *(name of assistant)* will give you a piece of paper that's that color. Red? Orange? Yellow? Green? Blue? Purple? *(Some colors may not be chosen by the children. Later, adults or teens can be asked to come forward to take the missing colors and participate at the end when a rainbow is made.)*

Now each of you has a favorite color in your hand. Let me ask you: when or where would you choose to use your favorite color? *(To paint my room. Buying a bike. Choosing a dress or shirt or other clothes.)*

Let's think about when you would not choose your favorite color. Everybody hold up the color that you chose again. I am going to ask you some questions. If you're answer is no, I want you to put your paper down by your side *(demonstrate)*.

Would you always choose your favorite color when eating M & M's? If your answer is "yes," keep your paper up; if "no," put your paper down. Now, let's start by having you all put your colors back up. Here we go.

Would you choose your favorite color to paint the walls in your bedroom? If not, put down your color.

Would you use your favorite color for the carpet or rugs on the floor in your bedroom? If yes, keep it up; if not, put it down. All put your colors back up.

If we were going to paint the walls here in church, would you like to see the church painted with your favorite color? If not, put your color down.

You can all put your colors down now. There are times when you wouldn't choose your favorite color. Let's think about why this is so. Too much of the same color would ruin the looks of things; we need many colors for things to look good.

Sharing so that other people get their favorite choice is also important. We each like different things, and each of us is important.

How about if we build a rainbow! You can use your favorite color to do that. Usually red is at the top, then orange and green in the middle, with blue and purple at the bottom. When you have found your place, hold up your color. We'll start with red on this end. (Designate where to go. Adults and youth willing to hold up the less-liked colors can join the children.)

Do you know how beautiful you look? Just like God intended a rainbow to look. And you look like a rainbow church, too. Using every color, Jesus wants us to build a rainbow church. Jesus wants us to include blondes and redheads, sandy-haired, black-haired, gray-haired, and bald-headed people, and people of all different skin colors, because that's the promise of the rainbow. It's one rainbow, but it has many colors. And the church around the world is one church but it has so many different kinds of people in it. That's what Jesus wants it to be. Thank you for all your help today.

(As the children leave, the congregation can join in singing "We Are the Church" by Avery and Marsh, especially the verse that begins "There are many kinds of people . . ." If that song is not available, find one that expresses the variety and unity of the church, perhaps "In Christ There Is No East or West," Lutheran Book of Worship, 359.) **–W.C.Y.**

The Day of Pentecost

The Gospel: John 14:8-17 (25-27)

Focus: Nobody has seen God, but when we see Jesus we know more about God. When we do the things that Jesus did, people will be able to see Jesus in us.

Experience: By talking about how others may see grandparents in children, children will learn to understand that people can also see Jesus in them, as people long ago saw God in Jesus.

Preparation: Bring photos of yourself and a grandparent or other relative that you resemble.

Believing Is Seeing

Good morning, boys and girls! Anybody ever tell you that you look like your grandmother or grandfather or another relative? How do they know that you look like that person? *(Responses. Be careful here if some children are adopted and don't know any biological relatives.)* Maybe they get out pictures of those people and compare your picture to theirs. People sometimes say that I look like my grandfather *(adapt to your situation)*. Let me put these two pictures next to each other. *(Show the pictures of yourself and a relative you look like.)* Or they can get me to stand next to that other person and notice the ways that we look a little bit alike, too *(name some: nose, smile, height, etc.)*

In Jesus' time they couldn't take pictures. Cameras hadn't been invented yet. They had to remember what people looked like or have the real person there in order to compare a child to a grandparent or another relative.

One day, Philip, a disciple of Jesus, told Jesus that he wanted to see God, his heavenly Father. Philip said that if he could just see God, he would be very happy. Jesus didn't have a scrapbook of pictures, but Jesus told Philip that he could get a picture of God by just watching him—not by looking at Jesus' hair, the shape of his nose, or the way he looked in his robe and sandals, but he could see God by watching what Jesus did. Philip could watch Jesus heal the sick, help the poor, tell adults the truth, and be friendly with children. When Jesus was good to people that others hated and taught people how to love and live, Philip would know just what God was like.

When Jesus was on earth, people could tell what God was like by watching what Jesus did. Now we are followers of Jesus, and do you know what? People are supposed to be able to see what Jesus is like by watching us! When we do good things, they are reminded of Jesus. What good things can we do? *(Responses. Visiting sick people, including other children when we play, being kind, not fighting, forgiving people, helping poor people.)* When we are loving and helpful and forgiving, we are like Jesus. Then others can know a little bit about Jesus.

Let's pray. Thank you, Jesus, for showing us that God is love. Help us to love the way you did so people will see what you are like when they watch us. Amen. **–W.C.Y.**

The Gospel: John 16:12-15

Focus: The love of God (Father, Son, and Holy Spirit) takes many different forms, and we are thankful for them all.

Experience: As the children look at pictures, they will identify things to be thankful for. Later you will read that list in the form of a prayer, using a refrain so that it becomes a litany.

Preparation: Bring three groups of pictures, with perhaps three pictures in each group (these are just suggestions): 1) For God as Creator, pictures of the natural world—animals, trees, people. 2) For God the Son, pictures of Jesus and the children, a cross, an Easter scene. 3) For God the Holy Spirit, pictures of people praying, a church, missionaries. Bring a pad of paper on which you have already written the items that the pictures show. Add additional comments from the children as you go along.

For These We Are Thankful

Good morning, kids. Today we are going to think about things we can thank God for. God loves us in so many ways and gives us so much. As we name what we see on some pictures I have here, I'll be sure they are written on my paper here. They will become a prayer of thankfulness to God that we'll pray later.

Let's look at the pictures I brought along. Here are some things God created. What are they? *(Show your first group of pictures of the created world, including people. The children can name what they see. Write down any responses that aren't already on your pad of things to be thankful for.)* God created everything in our world and God also created people: you and me and all those people! *(Point to the congregation.)* We are so thankful.

My next group of pictures are about Jesus. The best way to know how much God loves us in through Jesus. What are these pictures of? *(Go through your second set of pictures, have the children say what Jesus is doing, identify the cross and the resurrection if you were able to find an Easter scene. Again fill in any new responses on your pad.)* Jesus loved us so much that he died on the cross and then came alive again on Easter.

My last group of pictures shows quite a few things. They show how God is at work in our church and in the world. *(Go through your third set of pictures of the church, missionaries, etc. Prompt the children as needed to*

73

identify what each picture is about. Add their comments to your list.) God helps us pray, worship, and tell others that God loves them.

Now just look at my list here of all that we have named that God gives us and how God helps us. I will read them *(one item at a time or in groups)*, and then we will say, "Thank you, God!" *(As you read your list, the children could hold up the pictures for the items. After you say, for example, "For animals like deer and rabbits," you will say together, "Thank you, God!" You could add a summary prayer after each group of items, such as "For everything you created" for the first group, and "For Jesus' great love" for the second group, and "For all you do to help us know you" for the third group.)* Thank you all for helping me with this prayer. We really are thankful to God, aren't we. **–C.M.C.**

JUNE 14, 1998   JUNE 17, 2001   JUNE 13, 2004

The Gospel: Luke 7:36–8:3
Focus: We can show that we like someone in a lot of ways, even when that someone is Jesus.
Experience: Sharing ways people (and dogs) show they like someone, the children experience normal and strange ways that people express this feeling. They also learn that the strange ways the woman in the Gospel expressed her feelings were still acceptable too.
Preparation: Practice the story.

Jesus, I Like You

Good morning to you all. Do you like having a children's sermon when you get to sit up front together? *(Yes.)* I like children's sermons, too, because I like you! Tell me, what are some ways people can show you that they like you? *(Smile, hug, kiss, spend time with you, welcome you, etc. Show and do some of these.)* There are lots of ways to show someone we like them. How does a dog show you that he likes you? *(Wags tail, licks you.)* Those are good ways for a dog to show that he likes you. But what would you think if *I* licked your hand? Or sat in front of you with my hand on your leg, like a paw? *(Allow reactions.)* That would be strange, wouldn't it? Those ways are OK for a dog, but it would be strange for a person to act like that.

Once when Jesus was at a dinner in someone's house, a woman came in who liked Jesus very much. But do you know how she showed it? Do you know what she did? She cried until her tears fell on his feet. Then she wiped off his feet with her hair! Then she kissed his feet! Finally she poured expensive, perfumed oil on his feet. What do you think about that? *(Allow reactions.)* It does seem strange. But Jesus was very glad that she liked him so much. He didn't mind that she showed it in such a different way.

One of the best ways we can show Jesus that we like him is to talk to him often in prayer. Let's do that now. Jesus, we are so glad that you like us. Children were especially welcome around you. I pray that these children will always like you and always find a way to show you that they like you, by their prayers and by the way they live. Amen. **–C.M.C.**

Sunday between June 19-25 inclusive, Proper 7

JUNE 21, 1998   JUNE 24, 2001   JUNE 20, 2004

The Gospel: Luke 8:26-39

Focus: Saying Yes to the right things and No to the wrong things is an important lesson to learn.

Experience: The children will say Yes or No with their bodies as they respond to a list of situations and people that call for a decision.

Preparation: Make two large signs, one Yes, one No, which can be held by older youth or adult volunteers during the children's sermon. Put a green border on the Yes sign and a red one on the No sign. Develop a list with several items that require a choice on it. List "Jesus" last.

Yes or No

Hello, kids. I'm glad you came up today. I want you to help me show everyone the difference between Yes and No. *(Have volunteers stand about six feet apart and display the Yes and No signs.)* We often have to decide Yes or No about things. For instance, you said Yes, although maybe not out loud, when it was time to come forward for our time together, didn't you? *(Yes.)*

Today I will read a list of some things in our world. Children like you have to learn to say Yes or No to these things. Life is better when we say Yes to things that are good for us and No to things that can hurt us. Today you can show us what you decide by standing under one of these signs. Stand by the Yes sign, the green one, if you say Yes to what I read. Or if you decide No, stand by the No sign, the red one. Since all of you said Yes to coming forward for the children's sermon, why don't you all start under the Yes sign? *(Children stand and move under Yes sign.)* Now, every time I say something on my list, you decide to say Yes or No to it, and then go stand under the right sign. Here we go:

What do you say to drugs? *(Kids hopefully move to No sign.)* Good! I'm glad you say No to drugs. Next, what do you say to healthy food like carrots and apples and bread? Yes? That's a good choice. Next, what do you say to watching TV? *(Most will probably go to Yes.)* How about staying up late? *(Possible division of the house here.)* I see some of you by both signs. Some things in life are not always right or always wrong, are they? *(Continue with the list you have written until the final item.)* OK, here is another one:

What do you say to Jesus when he asks you to be his follower? You say Yes! That is wonderful! Today you have said Yes and No to many things.

In our Bible story today, Jesus said Yes and No. He said Yes to people who wanted him to leave their neighborhood. I think he thought it was OK to leave. And he said No to a man who wanted to go with him. He told him it was better to go home and tell people there about how good God was to him. Sometimes Jesus says No to us when we ask for things in our prayers. But Jesus always has a good reason to say No. It's like when our parents say, "No, you can't play in the street." They don't say No to be mean, but to keep us safe.

Still it is always good for us to say Yes to Jesus, because he loves us the best. Jesus always wants the best for us. So let's pray and thank Jesus for that.

Dear Jesus, we don't always like to be told No. When you tell us No, help us believe that you know what is best for us. May we always love you enough to keep saying Yes to you. Amen. **–C.M.C.**

Sunday between June 26—July 2 inclusive, Proper 8

JUNE 28, 1998   JULY 1, 2001   JUNE 27, 2004

The Gospel: Luke 9:51-62

Focus: Looking back can change a person's direction in walking or in following Jesus.

Experience: In an "experiment" format, the children will demonstrate what happens when they walk along a line of tape, first with their eyes looking forward, and then while looking backward. (This activity worked in practice; you may want to test it ahead of time with a few children yourself.)

Preparation: Somewhere near the spot where the children's sermon is given, stretch a 12 foot or longer line of masking tape on the floor or carpet. Keep it as straight as possible.

Walking the Line

Good morning, children. Today I want to have you do an experiment with me to demonstrate something that Jesus said. Our Bible lesson today tells us that Jesus "set his face" to go to Jerusalem. What do you think that means? *(They may not know; prompt them.)* Yes. Setting his face meant that Jesus was going to go right to Jerusalem, to keep going straight ahead and not get sidetracked, not get distracted or end up in another town. It was as if he could see Jerusalem at the end of a long, straight road, and he wasn't going to take his eyes off it until he got there.

So here is the experiment. I have put a long line of tape on the carpet here, like a long, straight road. I want you to walk on it twice. Who wants to go first? *(If they seem reluctant and no one child volunteers, let two or three children walk the line together, one after another.)* OK *(name)*, you wait here at one end of the line *(you go to other end)*. Now walk the line like Jesus, with your face set toward me. Look straight at me as you walk. *(Tell the child that is first in line to walk. Have her or him stop in front of you.)* Now look down. See? Your feet are right on the line. Why is that? *(Responses.)* Because your face was set forward, you stayed on the line. *(Repeat with other children as time allows.)*

Now let's change the experiment. This time you will try to walk the same line, but I will stand behind you. I want you to walk the line, but keep looking back at me. *(Demonstrate by walking a few steps with your head turned*

backward. Stand at the opposite end of the line. Have the first child look back at
you, then start walking the line. Tell him or her when to stop.) Now look down!
Your feet are not on the line, are they? You did not walk a very straight line
this time. Why not? *(Responses.)* You looked back! When you did not keep
your face set forward, you went off the line.

That's what Jesus meant! People who try to plow a straight line in a field
on a farm, or walk straight through life to heaven, can't do it if they keep
looking back. Because when we can't see where we are going, we go off the
straight line. The best way to go straight through life to heaven is to imagine
Jesus waiting for us there, just like I waited for you at the end of the line.
By doing that, every day we will keep remembering Jesus and praying to
him. Then we will do what Jesus wants us to do and show love to others,
because we will remember how much he loves us! **–C.M.C.**

Sunday between July 3-9 inclusive,
Proper 9

JULY 5, 1998   JULY 8, 2001   JULY 4, 2004

The Gospel: Luke 10:1-11, 16-20

Focus: The children learn the value of their names being written in heaven (verse 20) by seeing other places where names are written down.

Experience: The children will see names listed in various kinds of books. The benefit of names being written in these books will illustrate the blessing of our names being written in heaven.

Preparation: You will need an assortment of lists: a phone book, personal address book, church directory, Christmas list, team roster, cradle roll, etc. Try to find at least one with the children's names on it, or write up a list yourself.

The Best Place for a Name

(Greet the children by name, saying "Hi, (name)" and asking "And what is your name?" if new children are present.) We all have names, don't we? And our names can be written down in lots of places. Let me show you some of those places. *(Show phone book.)* Here is my name in the phone book. See? Now what good reasons can you think of to have my name written there? *(Allow responses or suggest answers.)* Here is another place with names. *(Show another list.)* Why is it good to have your name here? *(Allow responses. Proceed like this with other lists, being sure to use one with their names. If there are new children or some names are missing, write them in.)*

Well, kids, we have seen lots of places our names can be written. These are all good places. Where do you think Jesus said was the best place to have our names written? *(Responses. Help as needed.)* In heaven! So God must have a list of all the people who love God and believe in Jesus. That would be the best place of all, wouldn't it? Let's pray to Jesus about that.

Dear Jesus, we want our names to be written in the best place. We do believe in you, and we love you. We thank you that our names are writtin on your list in heaven. Amen. **–C.M.C.**

The Gospel: Luke 10:25-37
Focus: We can all look for ways to help our neighbors.
Experience: Hearing the story of the good Samaritan, the children are encouraged to think of someone whom they can help.
Preparation: Practice telling the story.

The Good Neighbor

(Greet the children.) Today let's talk about neighbors. Does anyone know what a neighbor is? (Allow or suggest answers, broadening their thinking to all people they meet, not just those living next door.) Who are some of your neighbors? (Allow responses.) Once Jesus told a man to love God and to love his neighbor. The man asked, "Who is my neighbor?" and Jesus told him a beautiful story. (Briefly tell the story of the good Samaritan from Luke 10:25-37: Man on a journey, robbed and left wounded, two men walked by and ignored him, good Samaritan stopped, bandaged his wounds, took him on his donkey to an inn, paid for his care. If time allows, as you tell the story, have some children pretend to be the man who was robbed, the robbers, the two people who walked by without helping, and the good Samaritan with his bandages and donkey.) That Samaritan was a very good neighbor, wasn't he? He was very helpful to the man who had been hurt and robbed.

Now we can learn from this story what it takes to for us to be good neighbors, too. Do you think you'd have to have a lot of bandages, money, and a donkey? That's what the good neighbor in the story had. (No.) Do you think that if you don't have these things, you can't be a good neighbor? (No.) That's good. Because you can be a good neighbor in many ways. All you really need is to help someone who needs help.

So, answer these questions for me. Do you need a lot of bandages? (No!) Money? (No!) Do you need a donkey? (No!) Of course not. You don't even have to be grown-up. You just need someone you can help. It might be a lonely person who would be cheered up by a visit from you. Or it could be a sick person who would enjoy a picture that you drew. There are many ways to be a good neighbor. I hope this week you can find someone who needs you to be a good neighbor to them. What do you think you could do this week to help someone? (Responses. Try to get several to say what they can do.) So you can be a good Samaritan and help others even if you don't have a donkey! **–C.M.C.**

Sunday between July 17-23 inclusive,
Proper 11

The Gospel: Luke 10:38-42

Focus: The busyness of preparation is contrasted with the simplicity of welcome.

Experience: The children observe a would-be Guest knocking at the door (staged) who is kept waiting by a person who wants to get everything ready first. Then a second person simply welcomes the Guest inside. The contrast is drawn to illustrate "choosing the better part": receiving Jesus.

Preparation: Select two or three volunteers (adults or teens with loud voices), give them copies of this skit, and rehearse it prior to Sunday. Stage it to maximize visibility for the children and the congregation.

Knock, Knock!

(Greet the children.) Today we are going to see a little skit and learn a very important lesson. *(Tell the children the names of the persons who will be the Guest, Busy Person, and Welcomer; you might choose to be one of them yourself.)* Let's watch and listen.

GUEST: *(speaks)* Knock, Knock! *(Busy Person pretends to open door.)*

BUSY PERSON: Oh, hello! Oh, my, I wasn't expecting you so early. The house is such a mess. Just let me straighten up a little. Why don't you wait out here for a little while. *(Shuts the door, then pantomimes sweeping floor, dusting, etc.)*

GUEST: Knock, knock ! *(Busy Person opens door a second time.)*

BUSY PERSON: Oh, it's you again. Really, just let me get myself ready. *(Shuts the door, then pantomines combing hair, brushing teeth, or putting on a jacket or shoes.)*

GUEST: *(In a loud voice)* Knock! Knock ! *(Busy Person opens door a third time.)*

BUSY PERSON: I'm so sorry to keep you waiting, but now I have to run to the store and get a few things for us to eat for lunch. I'll be right back. *(After busy person leaves, Guest shrugs shoulders and goes to another door.)*

GUEST: Knock, Knock! *(Welcomer opens door.)*

WELCOMER: Oh *(name of person)*, what a nice surprise! *(Hugs the Guest.)* Come in and sit down! It's so good to see you! Tell me how you are. *(Guest and Welcomer pretend to talk together.)*

Wonderful! Thank you very much for helping with that play. *(The people return to their seats.)* Now, kids, who made the Guest feel welcome, the first person or the second? *(The second one.)* What did *(he/she)* do to welcome the Guest? *(Invited the Guest in, hugged him or her, etc.)* What did the first person do instead of welcoming the Guest? *(Cleaned the house, changed clothes, and went out to get groceries, leaving the Guest standing outside.)*

Our Bible lesson today tells about a time when something like this happened to Jesus. It's nice to be all cleaned up and have a neat house and a special meal. But Jesus said all he really needed was to feel welcome, the way *(name of Welcomer)* welcomed *(name of Guest)* in our skit.

I know that you hear in Sunday school or church that Jesus wants you to be his follower. He wants to come into your heart. Some people might say, "I'm too busy right now." But others say, "Jesus, I'm glad you love me. I love you, too. Please come in." I hope that's what you children will do— ask Jesus to come into your heart and to feel welcome in your home and wherever you are. And I know that would make Jesus very happy. **–C.M.C.**

Sunday between July 24-30 inclusive, Proper 12

The Gospel: Luke 11:1-13
Focus: We are to pray boldly.
Experience: The children hear a story about Megan who asked a good neighbor for something and learn that they can ask God for what they need.
Preparation: Practice the story.

Megan Learns to Ask

(Greet the children.) Jesus once told his disciples, "Ask, and it will be given to you; seek, and you will find; knock, and it will be opened to you."

Can any of you think about a time when you wanted something very, very much but wondered if you dare ask for it? Tell me about it. *(Responses. Wanted a certain toy for Christmas, to go to summer camp, a particular shoes.)* Why were you afraid to ask? *(Parents might get mad, too expensive, family just paid lots of money for trip, family member sick, etc.)*

Today we're going to hear about Megan, who lived next door to Mrs. Marple, who had an apple tree in her back yard. When Megan went out to play, she'd watch those apples growing bigger and redder all summer. She just loved apples and wished she could have one. They looked so juicy and sweet. She even thought about climbing over the fence and stealing one.

One day Megan's mother saw her looking up at Mrs. Marple's apple tree. She could just about imagine what Megan was thinking. What do you think Megan was thinking? *(I want an apple. I wish she's give me one.)* And that's what Megan told her mother.

So her mother said, "Megan, why don't you just go and ask for one?" Megan was shy, so she answered, "I don't dare ask Mrs. Marple." Her mother said, "Why not? She's a kind woman and loves all you children."

"I know, Mom, but I feel afraid." Why do you think Megan was afraid? *(She had trouble talking to grown-ups, wouldn't know how to ask.)* That's just what Megan said. She didn't know how to ask.

That's the way we are with God. We know God loves us very, very much. God has even told us to ask and we will receive. But still we're bashful and shy. Let's listen to what Jesus tells us in the Bible. Jesus said, "Ask, and it will be given you; search, and you will find; knock, and the door will be opened." Let's say Jesus' words together. *(Say each phrase again and have the children repeat each one after you.)*

Megan's mom said, "I'll go with you while you ring the doorbell. When Mrs. Marple answers the door, just tell her, "I'd really like one of the apples from your tree. May I please have one?"

They walked together over to her house. Mrs. Marple opened the door and smiled. Megan smiled back and said confidently, "I'd really like one of the apples from your tree. May I please have one?" What do you think happened? *(She said "yes," glad she'd asked, glad to see her, said come any time and have another.)* Mrs. Marple liked Megan. She was so happy Megan had asked. She was glad to give Megan an apple and told her she could have more at other times. All she needed to do was come and ask.

Jesus said we should ask. Let's fold our hands. Dear God, we know that you love us very, very much. And we love you very, very much. You have told us to ask and we will receive. So let's each of us say what we need from God, either out loud or in our hearts. *(Responses. Grandpa get well, presents for my birthday, dad find a job.)* Thank you, dear God, for hearing and answering us. Amen. **–C.C.**

The Gospel: Luke 12:13-21

Focus: Selfishness destroys us, but Jesus is able to make us thankful and generous.

Experience: The children will hear and watch the story of the farmer who only thought about his riches. The children will feel the sorrow of stinginess and the joy of sharing.

Preparation: Make five rough-drawn crayon pictures: 1) a little red bulging barn with tremor lines as though it is about to burst, 2) open land, a field, with a big, yellow sun shining above it, 3) fat, blue rain drops, and 4) a very large red barn.

The Stingy Farmer

(Greet the children.) Jesus taught us that we cannot be happy if we pile up money and things to keep all for ourselves without giving any back to God or to other people. But sometimes it's hard to share. Can you think of a time when you did not want to share? (Candy, seat by the window on our trip.) We all know what it's like to feel selfish and not want to share. Big people are like that, too. All of us. It's quite natural. But selfishness hurts us. So we all need help from Jesus to become thankful and generous. To help us, Jesus told us this story.

A farmer had a little red barn (hold up picture of small barn). He worked very hard to plant his wheat in the soil and it grew because God made the sun shine (picture of field with sun shining). God made rain to fall, watering the wheat (picture of raindrops) to make the plants grow. I can imagine this farmer being so thankful to God for all God gave—the wheat seeds, the soil, the sun, and the rain. I'm sure he said a thank-you prayer to God every time he and his family sat down to eat.

What thank you prayer do you think they said. Maybe the one you say? What mealtime prayers do you say at your house? ("Come Lord Jesus, be our guest, and let these gifts to us be blest," or others. Add your own favorite if different from the following.) My favorite prayer at mealtime is, "God is great; God is good; And we thank him for our food. By his hand we all are fed. Give us, Lord, our daily bread. Amen." It's important to keep saying thank-you prayers to God so we remember all that God does for us.

I think this farmer went to worship every Sunday with his family, too, just as you all are here today. Important things happen here in church. Can you tell me what some of those important things are that we do here Sunday morning? *(Think about what God does for us, thank and praise God, listen to readings and sermons, sing, pray for people in need, give gifts.)* Yes, we need to stay close to God. The farmer did at first, but then listen to what happened.

His fields grew so much wheat. He put it into the little red barn, and it got so full it nearly burst *(show picture of small barn).* So he tore it down and built a new large barn *(show picture of large barn).* He worked hard every day. He got too busy to say thank you prayers at mealtime and too busy to go to worship on Sundays. He forgot all the ways God helped him. He wasn't thankful anymore. He complained a lot, forgot about poor and hungry people God wanted him to help, and didn't give gifts back to God anymore. There was no smile on his face anymore. He got grumpy and sad and stingy.

Do you think Jesus is able to make this farmer thankful and happy and generous again? *(Nod yes, children nod yes).* Yes, it is only Jesus who is able to make all of us thankful and generous. Let's ask Jesus to help us be thankful. Please fold your hands while we pray. Dear Jesus, help us every day to be filled with thanks to you for all that we have. Help us to share what we have. Amen. **–C.C.**

The Gospel: Luke 12:32-40

Focus: We trust God and respond to God by helping others.

Experience: By listening to Jenna's question and her mother's answer, the children will learn about trust.

Preparation: Practice the story.

Jenna Learns Trust

(Greet the children.) On the way home from church one Sunday, Jenna said to her mother, "In Sunday school today we learned a Bible verse, 'Trust in the Lord, and do good.' * Mom, what does trust mean?"

Does anyone here know what "trust" means? How would you have answered Jenna? *(Prompt as needed. You can believe what a person says, you're not afraid of them, you feel good around them.)* Those are good answers. Would you like to hear how Jenna's mother explained what trust is?

Jenna's mother thought for a minute and then said, "Jenna, do you remember how when you were smaller you liked to play the game of jump-off-the-table?"

"Wheeee," Jenna said, as she scrambled to put a chair over by the kitchen counter top. Quick as a wink she was up there, spreading out her arms as though she was going to fly! And as her mother had always done before, she stood ready, reaching out. "Jump, Jenna," she said.

Just like that Jenna jumped into her mother's waiting arms, giggling as she landed. Her mother squeezed her and laughed as she asked, "Jenna, weren't you afraid to jump?"

"No! I knew you wouldn't let me get hurt!"

"Jenna," her mother said, "you believed I would catch you just as I've always done before. That is trust. You trusted me to take care of you. You knew I wouldn't let you get hurt. You believed I'd take good care of you. God is like that. He loves us so much. We can trust God. Because we are thankful for that, we look for ways to do good. That's what God wants. We can be God's helpers by loving and taking care of others who need help."

Jenna's mother is right. We are thankful we can trust God, and we want

* Psalm 37:3a

to help others. How about each of you? What can you do to help others? *(Be kind to sisters or brothers, help a new kid in school, obey parents, bring food for the food shelf, other examples.)*

Let's pray about this. Please fold your hands while we pray. Dear God, we are thankful we can trust you to love us, care for us, and help us. Each day show us how we can help others. Amen. **–C.C.**

Sunday between August 14-20 inclusive, Proper 15

AUG. 16, 1998   AUG. 19, 2001   AUG. 15, 2004

The Gospel: Luke 12:49-56

Focus: We are wise to follow Jesus faithfully.

Experience: The children will think about running a race and how that is like following Jesus every day.

Preparation: Bring a running shoe in a bag or box.

Running a Race

(Greet the children.) Jesus wants all of us to follow him. Every day Jesus wants us to obey him. Sometimes that's very hard, especially when a good friend tries to talk you into doing something you know you shouldn't do. Has that ever happened to you? *(Responses. I went to my friend's house and my parents didn't know where I was. I decided not to let someone play with my friend and me. I was mean to someone my friend doesn't like.)* We've all done things that we've known we shouldn't do. What do you feel like afterward when you think about what you did? *(Feel bad, wish I hadn't done it.)* Maybe we think it's not too serious at first, but later we're very sorry.

Well, Jesus tells us that it can be hard to follow him, hard to be obedient to him. It can be hard for children, but it can be hard for big people, like moms and dads, too.

Today I have a shoe here *(take running shoe out of the bag or box).* When would you wear a shoe like this? *(For playing, hiking, running.)* Yes, you could wear this shoe when you're playing or hiking. One of you said it would be good for running. You could wear it when you run in a race. Who can tell me what a race is? *(People run to a finish line, there's a winner, everyone tries to finish the race.)* What do you think it feels like to run in a race? *(Get tired, feel like you want to quit, get thirsty.)* Yes, you do get tired and thirsty. You might even feel like quitting. But there are helpers at a race. Lots of people come to watch and cheer for the runners. When the people shout and cheer it makes the runners feel sure they can make it to the end and even win!

Jesus tells us that following Jesus is like running a race. We can obey Jesus because we have lots of help. So we can all be winners. There are lots of people cheering us on, including people who loved Jesus and have gone to heaven. Who do you know who loved Jesus and has gone to heaven?

(Ask, "Who has died?" if they don't understand.) (Responses. Grandpa, aunt, little sister.) The Bible tells us that they are all watching us and cheering for us while we live our life. When they're cheering us on it will help us to obey Jesus. We can cheer for each other. We can encourage each other to be obedient to God every day.

And there's someone else who's watching and helping us. It's Jesus. He was a child like you. And he became a grown-up like your mom and dad. When he was tempted to do bad things, Jesus asked God to help him. That's how Jesus was always able to be obedient. Jesus understands you. And he is watching you and always cheers you on so you will do the right thing.

What are some right things you know God wants you to do? *(Be nice to my sister or brother, help at home, be nice to people who are sad.)* Yes, those are important things we know God wants us to do. But sometimes, we're not really sure what the right things are. What do we do then? *(Prompt as needed. Pray, Talk to Mom or Dad or others for advice, ask God to show us.)* Yes, remember that we can always pray to God and ask for help when we don't know what to do. Let's do that right now.

Let's fold our hands and pray. Dear Jesus, you always did what God wanted. Help us every day to do the good things you want us to do. Amen.
–C.C.

Sunday between August 21-27 inclusive, Proper 16

AUG. 23, 1998   AUG. 26, 2001   AUG. 22, 2004

The Gospel: Luke 13:22-30
Focus: We learn about the way into God's kingdom.
Experience: Standing in a circle, the children will hold hands tightly to keep others out until two of them make a door so those outside can enter. They'll learn that Jesus is the only way for us to enter the kingdom of God.
Preparation: Practice the story.

How Do I Get In?

(Greet the children.) Jesus often talked to people about the kingdom of God. What do you think of when you hear the word kingdom? *(Responses. A land where a king rules. Hear about kingdoms in stories in TV shows, movies, and fairy tales.)*

Jesus teaches us in the Bible about his kingdom. You can't really see his kingdom but you can belong to it. In our Bible lesson today Jesus tells us how we can get into his kingdom, how we can belong to it. Jesus said, "I am the door." What does a door do? *(Responses. It lets people into a house or a building or a room. It can keep you out, it can keep you in.)* Those are all very good ideas.

We're going to play a game called, "How Do I Get in?" Let's stand and make a circle. We'll need most of you to help me make our circle. Two of you *(ask for volunteers or choose two who have good self-esteem)* are going to try to get inside the circle.

OK, let's hold hands to make a tight fence. Let's pretend we have an amusement park inside of our circle and these two *(say their names)* really want to get in. What might we have in our amusement park here? *(Ferris wheel, bumper cars, water slide, other responses.)* They're going to try real hard to get through our fence! First they'll try to break the fence down. *(The two children try.)* That didn't work. They're going to try to crawl over the fence. *(They try.)* That didn't work either. So next, they're going to try to crawl under the fence. *(They try.)* But nothing works! The only way they'll get in is if a door opens.

Jesus said, "I am the door." Jesus lets us into his kingdom. Let's have *(choose two children making the circle) (name)* and *(name)* be the door. Can you open your door and invite those two children inside the park? *(The two door children say, "Come in" and open the door. The children on the outside walk in.)* Now that they've found the door, they have a whole lot of freedom. They can go out and come back in as they choose because they know who to ask. *(If time allows, let others take turns being outside, going to the door children, asking to come in, and getting in.)*

Jesus said, "I am the door." Remember we can't get into Jesus' kingdom by forcing our way in. But we can get in easily by asking, because he is kind and opens the door for us. If we ask him, he let us in his kingdom. He loves us so much, and we love him, too, don't we? *(Yes.)*

Let's review what Jesus said: "I am the *(_____)." (Door).* That's right. Jesus loves us and welcomes us into his kingdom, and that's where we want to be. Let's fold our hands and pray. Dear Jesus, thank you for including us in your kingdom. We know you love us, and we love you, too! Amen.

–C.C.

Sunday between August 28—September 3 inclusive, Proper 17

The Gospel: Luke 14:1, 7-14
Focus: Jesus tells a story about not trying to be first and he encourages us to be humble and work together instead of being first.
Experience: By forming a line, the children will experience the urge to be first. When they form a circle, they can visualize the equality and teamwork that Jesus calls us to.
Preparation: Make sure you have adequate floor space for this activity.

Together around Jesus

(Greet the children.) A long time ago when I was much smaller and was in kindergarten, all of us kindergarten students would line up when we had to leave our classroom. We would make a long line in the hallway before we went to recess or before we went to the lunchroom. Let's try lining up like that today. Please stand up and make a line. *(Allow time for this.)*

That is a good line. Now, something I remember from kindergarten was that there were a couple of students who always wanted to be first in line. "Me first, me first!" they would shout as they pushed their way up to the front of the line *(you may act this out as you describe it)*. That was not very nice. Those students didn't want to take turns in line. They always wanted to be first.

Jesus talks to us about always wanting to be first. While we hear about that, I would like all of you to sit down right where you are. Please sit down so we are all sitting in our line. *(After the children are seated, continue.)* In the Bible, Jesus tells us a story about people who came to a wedding dinner. Some of the people sat in the best places. They wanted to be first in line for the food and all the attention. But they really got a surprise when they found out that they could not be first and they had to move to other chairs.

Jesus tells us this story so that we will hear that we should not try to always be first, first in line or first for the food. Jesus says that it will be better if we don't worry about being first and instead let others have a turn at being first. Jesus wants us to work together.

You can help me show everyone today what Jesus wants. Would you all please stand up again right where you are *(children stand)*. Now, please turn this way *(indicate that the children are to face right)*. Who is first in line now?

(Let children say the child's name or describe him or her.) Now, please turn around and face this way *(the children face left)*. Who is first in line now? *(Let the children say child's name or describe him or her.)* Good! That is one way to take turns being first.

Now let's really change things around. Let's form a circle. *(Allow time and movement.)* Great! Now who is first? Who is last? *(Nobody is. Other responses.)* We could say no one is first or last or everyone is first and last. This circle is nice because we are all together and we are not fighting over who is first or last. And if we had to go somewhere we could take turns letting different people lead us out. We could really work together. A circle can help us remember that Jesus wants us to work together.

Let's keep holding hands and close our eyes and pray about that right now. Dear Jesus, help us not to fight about being first. Help us to take turns being first and to work together. Amen. **–J.B.S.**

SEP. 6, 1998   SEP. 9, 2001   SEP. 5, 2004

The Gospel: Luke 14:25-33

Focus: Jesus calls us to think about what it means for us and our lives to be his followers.

Experience: Through the use of toy blocks and the building of two separate towers, the children learn about what goes into building a block tower and in building their lives around Jesus.

Preparation: You will need a few wooden blocks or toy logs for the first tower. Put them in a bag. If you are working on carpet, bring a board for a firm base. Bring a picture of Jesus large enough for your group to see clearly. For the second tower you need six "blocks" (cans of soup are sturdy and stack well). Prepare these six labels and tape one on each can: pray, share, forgive, help, give, and love. *Optional:* a table to put the six cans on. *(Note:* If time is short, omit the first tower-building activity and move directly to the tower made of cans.)

Building on Jesus

(Greet the children.) Today I have some building blocks with me and I'm going to build a tower. Watch me, because here I go. *(Dump the blocks or whatever you brought into a heap on the floor but don't build anything.)* Well, what do you think of my tower? *(Responses. They will probably say it's not much of a tower.)* Maybe it's not really a very good tower, after all. It's not very high and it's a bit of a mess. But it sure was quick to build!

Maybe I should have taken more time to think about it and then build it. What if I did this? *(Pause, thinking, and then take one block at a time and build a better tower but keep it simple to save time. Use a board as a base if you are working on carpet.)* There, that is better! This time I took my time and built a better tower.

In our Bible reading today, Jesus talks about building a tower. He says that if you are going to build a tower out of blocks or anything else, it is good to think about it first. Then Jesus says that if you and I are going to listen to him and follow him, it is good to think about that first, too. So, just as we think about how to build a good tower out of blocks (point to block tower), it is also good to think about how to follow Jesus. We think about what Jesus says (hold up picture of Jesus) and what we do when we listen to Jesus. *(Gather up the blocks from the first tower and put them in the bag.)*

You can help me do that this morning. I have something else to build with this morning *(point to the labelled soup cans)*. Can anyone read the labels on these cans? *(Wait for responses or read them yourself: pray, share, forgive, help, give, love.)*

Good! All of these things are what followers of Jesus do. I need six helpers *(choose from those who volunteer)*. You will be helping us build a new tower. *(As you refer to the name on each "block" or soup can, ask the children to be ready to move the cans into place.)*

We talk to Jesus when we say our prayers *(have a child put' the "pray" soup can in place)*. We share our toys with others *(have second child put the "share" soup can next to it)*. We forgive other people when they say they are sorry. Jesus doesn't want us to stay mad at each other all the time *(third child puts the "forgive" soup can in the row with the other two)*. We help other people. If someone is lonely on the playground, we ask them to play with us. If someone falls and hurts their knee, we find a teacher or helper for them *(fourth child puts the "help" soup can on top of the row of three cans)*. Followers of Jesus also give. We give our money to help hungry people. We give our time to learn about Jesus in Sunday school *(fifth child puts the "give" soup can next to the "help" one)*. Jesus also asks us to love God and each other. We are doing that right now this morning when we sing and pray to God in church *(sixth child puts the "love" soup can at top of tower)*. And we love others when we do these others things *(gesture toward the first five soup cans and read the words on them)*.

We have built a very fine tower by thinking about how to follow Jesus. Jesus will help you and me do these things, too *(place the picture of Jesus near the tower)*. Jesus is with us when we pray, share, forgive, help, give, and love. That is really good news. Thank you for helping me talk about Jesus and build this good tower this morning. **–J.B.S.**

Sunday between September 11-17 inclusive, Proper 19

The Gospel: Luke 15:1-10
Focus: When the lost is found, we rejoice and celebrate.
Experience: The use of a sign allows the children to know the joy felt by the shepherd, the woman, and God at the finding of what was lost.
Preparation: Make a sign large enough for children to read which reads: "Yeah! Welcome Back!" Find a picture of a shepherd and sheep (or a picture of Jesus) and a play money bill of $100 (or make your own).

Yeah! Welcome Back!

(Greet the children.) I have a sign with some words written on it. Can someone who already goes to school read it for me please? *(Hold up the sign and wait for responses.)* Thank you. Now let's think about these words. When I say, "Yeah!" *(say it with joy),* what do you think I am feeling? *(Responses.)* Yes, all those feelings could be true. And when I say "Welcome back!" *(again say it with joy and warmth, perhaps hold out your arms in welcome),* what do you think I am feeling? *(You may get similar responses. You could respond by saying, "Yes, some of the same feelings as with the word 'yeah.' Only this time I want the person to know how special she is and how happy I am that she is back.")*

Let's practice saying these words together when I hold up the sign *(hold up the sign for group and practice saying the words).* Good! Now every time I hold up the sign be sure to say those words.

In our Bible story Jesus tells us about a shepherd who lost one sheep *(hold up a picture of a shepherd and sheep, or a picture of Jesus, telling the children Jesus is like a good shepherd).* The shepherd went out hunting for the lost sheep in hills and rocks, in long grass and bushes, and finally found it. The shepherd was really happy. He said something like this *(hold up sign and let children respond).* Good!

Jesus also tells us about a woman who lost a silver coin. It was worth at least $100 of our money today *(hold up $100 bill of play money and then put it behind you or under something nearby, maybe under a Bible or hymnbook, as if it is lost).* When the woman knew it was lost, she looked and looked for it. She cleaned the whole house, hunting for it, and when she finally found it *(find the play money),* she said something like this *(hold up sign and let children respond).* That's right!

Jesus wants us to listen to these stories because we don't just lose sheep or money. We can lose people, too. I'll tell you a story to show you what Jesus means.

There was a Sunday school class that had many boys and girls in it. One boy named Pete liked to come, but he also missed a lot of classes. One time he missed a whole bunch and even missed the Sunday school Christmas program. The next time he came back to Sunday school, he was a little afraid that the other children might say bad things about him.

I know what Jesus would like us to say to Pete if we were in his Sunday school class (hold up sign and encourage children to respond with "Yeah! Welcome back!").

Sometimes people can be like lost sheep or lost coins (point to the picture and to the play money). We can be away from Sunday school or church for a while. Jesus says that we are all still important and when we are found or when we come back, everyone can be happy. So we can say (hold up sign and let children respond, "Yeah! Welcome back!") with Jesus, because Jesus is celebrating with us, too. **–J.B.S.**

Sunday between September 18-24 inclusive, Proper 20

SEP. 20, 1998   SEP. 23, 2001   SEP. 19, 2004

The Gospel: Luke 16:1-13

Focus: God calls each of us to be a good manager of our talents in order to do God's work.

Experience: Through talking about the word "manager" and its meaning, the children learn that they are managers who do God's work. A name tag helps each child remember he or she is a manager.

Preparation: Make a name tag for yourself with "Manager *(followed by your first name)*" on it. Bring enough blank name tags (peel off, self-adhesive would be best) for all the children, with the word "Manager" written on each ahead of time. During the children's sermon, have an adult or older teen write each child's name on a name tag so that each tag will say "Manager *(the child's name)*." These will be handed out at the end of the sermon.

We Are God's Managers

(Greet the children.) This morning I would like us to think about a story Jesus told us in the Bible. Jesus started the story out by saying that there was a rich man who had a manager, and he found out that his manager was messing things up, not taking good care of his property or his money.

Do you know what a manager is? *(Responses. They may not know.)* If someone was the manager of a store, what kinds of things would that person do? *(Help the children think of answers: Order things to sell in the store, keep track of the money, take it to the bank, be honest, do what the boss says, other responses.)* Jesus' story is about a manager who wasted the boss's money. Jesus tells us this story because you and I are managers of all God has given us. Jesus doesn't want us to waste the good things God has given us.

See what I'm wearing this morning *(point to your name tag)*. My friend _____ *(name)* will be asking your names as we go along in order to write them down, but keep listening to me, too. My name tag says that I'm "Manager _____ *(your first name)*." I'm a manager because God has given me things to do. God has given all of us things to do. For instance, people who like to sing, sing in our church choir. God has given them a talent for singing, so they use it in church.

Can you help me think of other ways people do God's work and help others? What do we see people doing in church and for the church, and for other people? *(Possible responses are singing, praying, giving money, teaching Sunday school, playing the organ or piano, bringing food for the food pantry, helping neighbors, visiting sick people, recycling.)* Those are all good things people do. You do many of those things, too. When you and I use our voices and hands to help others, we are good managers. God has given us lots of talents. God has given us our voices *(you and children point to mouths)*, our good minds *(all point to heads)* for thinking, our feet for running errands and helping people *(all step in place)*, and our hands for praying *(all fold hands)*, helping *(pretend to cook food or wash something, saying what you are doing; the children can do it, too)*, and hugging *(all wrap arms around themselves)*.

Think about what good things you can do with your voice, your mind, your feet, and your hands. Remember you are God's manager. To help you remember that today, we have a special name tag for each of you today *(get completed name tags from your helper and hand them out, calling off each name saying, "Manager (child's name)." Hand out all tags and have your helper assist you if it is a large group)*. You are a great bunch of managers!

Now, let's close our eyes and fold our hands and talk to God before we go. Dear God, thank you for making each one of us managers. Help us to use our voices, minds, feet, and hands to help other people. Amen. **–J.B.S.**

Sunday between September 25—October 1 inclusive, Proper 21

SEP. 27, 1998   SEP. 30, 2001   SEP. 26, 2004

The Gospel: Luke 16:19-31
Focus: Jesus calls us to give generously when we help others.
Experience: The example of the two cans of food helps children visualize a leftover gift and a more generous gift, and then apply this to helping others.
Preparation: Find a small can of spinach (or other vegetable that does not appeal to most children) and a large can of spaghetti and meatballs (or other food that does appeal to most children). Find a picture of Lazarus in a Bible storybook if you can.

Give More than Leftovers

(Greet the children.) This morning I have two different cans of food. *(Hold up the cans.)* Can you tell what's in this can? *(Responses. Spinach.)* And in this big one? *(Responses. Spaghetti and meatballs.)* Which do you like best? *(Responses.)* Well, I like spinach *(or whatever food you brought),* but I have to admit that if I was really hungry I would want this big can of spaghetti and meatballs *(or whatever food you brought).*

I brought these cans today because I want you think about something. What if some people from *(use the name of a group that does a food drive such as scouts or church)* collected food to give to hungry people, and all they collected were tiny cans of vegetables like this tiny can of spinach? Do you think the hungry people would be very happy? *(Responses.)* Vegetables are good for us, but it would be hard to have just spinach to eat. But it's a good thing that many people are willing to give a lot of other kinds of food, like this big can of spaghetti and meatballs, or big cans of beef stew, chowmein, canned ham, and lots more. Those cans of food would help feed lots of people, wouldn't they? *(Yes.)*

Jesus tells us a story in the Bible today about a very hungry and poor person named Lazarus *(hold up picture of Lazarus if you found one).* Lazarus was very hungry but a rich man wouldn't help him very much at all. The rich man just gave Lazarus little bits of food, just the leftovers. That is something like giving only one small can of vegetables, ones we don't like, to the food drive. It's like leftovers. It isn't enough for a hungry person to fill up on. Lazarus was always hungry. The leftover food from the rich man was not enough.

Jesus tells us this story to make you and me think about how we help others. Do we help just a little bit, enough to get by, or do we do something that will really help the person? *(Hold up the large can of spaghetti and meatballs.)* Jesus wants us to help people with what they need. Sometimes that means giving very big cans of good food so hungry people will have enough to eat, or money to those who buy big cases full of food for the food shelf.

Sometimes we can help people in other ways. How would you help a friend who had just knocked all his or her toys *(or blocks, markers, crayons)* on the floor by accident. Would you just say, "Oh, that's too bad," and walk away, or would you go over and help your friend pick up the toys? *(Responses.)* We could do either one, but helping pick things up would really help our friend.

Jesus wants us to be helpers like this because he loves all of us. He loves poor people and he loves rich people. He loves boys and he loves girls. He loves children and he loves grown-ups. When we help other people and give them more than just leftovers, we are sharing Jesus' love with them.

Let's close our eyes and fold our hands and talk to God about that. Dear God, thank you for loving all of us. Help us to be willing to give lots of food to those who are hungry and to help people when they need our help. Amen. **—J.B.S.**

The Gospel: Luke 17:5-10

Focus: Jesus calls us to serve God and teaches us not to expect special rewards for the service we do.

Experience: By thinking of the teamwork needed to play a game, the children can begin to see the church as God's team, which needs all people to participate regardless of reward.

Preparation: You will need a piece of tagboard (or large sheet of paper) and a marker.

We Are on God's Team

(Greet the children.) This morning I would like us to think about some of our favorite games to play, some outside ones, some to play inside. Let's make a list *(hold up tagboard and marker)*. What are some of your favorites? *(Write down all responses.)*

This is a great list. I played some of these games when I was your age, too. I remember that they were the most fun when everyone played together without fighting. That is important in a game like baseball *(or choose another game that has been listed by the children)*. In a baseball game we need lots of players who do different things. One pitches the ball, other players take turns hitting the ball, some players play way out in the outfield, and others stand near the bases.

What would it be like if in a baseball game the pitcher said, "I won't throw the ball to you unless you give me something first!" Or, what would it be like if the person who hits the ball with the bat said to the rest of the team, "I'll hit a home run if you promise to give me lots of money." *(Responses.)* Pretty soon the game wouldn't be much fun, and there might even be fighting. If the players thought only about what prize or treat or money they would get, the game wouldn't be fun anymore.

Jesus tells us that you and I are on a team. We are on God's team. That is very special. Each one of you *(gesture toward the children)* is on God's team. God knows your name. God loves you, and God has things for you to do. God wants you and everyone here this morning to work together. We can pray for other people. We can sing together, and we can help other people.

I wonder what would happen if all of a sudden the people here *(gesture all around the congregation)* started saying things like this: *I won't pray unless you give me some money (make a stubborn face).* I won't come to church unless you do a special favor for me *(cross arms and look determined).* I won't go to Sunday school unless you buy me a candy bar *(put hands on hips).* That wouldn't be very nice. We would be asking for a reward or treat for everything we do. Soon all we would hear is "Gimme, gimme, gimme!"

Jesus wants you and me to remember that we are on God's team. The things that we do, like singing, praying, coming to church and Sunday school, and helping, we do because we love God. We don't have to be paid or given special treats to do them. We just do what we ought to,* as Jesus says in the Bible. That is real teamwork! And it is a lot more fun.

Let's talk to God about that by closing our eyes and folding our hands. Dear God, thank you that you love us and we are on your team. Help us all to pray, sing, and work together because we love you. Amen. **—J.B.S.**

* Luke 17:10b

The Gospel: Luke 17:11-19

Focus: Jesus deserved thanks from the ten lepers he healed.

Experience: In acting out the story of the ten lepers, the children experience the story and say thanks to Jesus.

Preparation: Find a picture of Jesus for one child to hold. Purchase or make a number of white stick-on dots (you'll need about three per child) to put on the children who will pretend they are lepers. Recruit an assistant in advance to help you put on and take off the dots if you have a large group of children.

Thank You, Jesus!

(Greet the children.) Today I would like your help in acting out a story from the Bible. First let's divide our group in half. *(If group is large, have one group of ten and the rest in the second group. It's OK if both groups are smaller than ten each.)* Now, would someone volunteer to be Jesus? *(Give the volunteer a picture of Jesus to hold and have the child stand between the two groups.)*

This group *(you or your assistant go to the group of ten or less and begin putting white dots on the children's arms and hands).* Will be the people who pretend they have leprosy. Does anyone know what leprosy is? *(Responses. Prompt as needed.)* Yes, it is a sickness that you see on the skin. These white dots will help us pretend that these children are lepers. Leprosy was a very bad disease and it was very serious. People were afraid of it and afraid of getting it.

What I would like this group over here to do *(the observers)* is to show us with their faces how people who were afraid of these lepers *(gesture to the group of children with the dots on their skin)* would look. *(Encourage and demonstrate looks of fear, hands in front of faces, even stepping back away from lepers.)* That's good!

Now one day Jesus *(gesture to volunteer)* was on his way to Jerusalem and the lepers saw him and said, "Have mercy on us!" Will you children who are pretending to be lepers please show us your sad faces while you say, "Have mercy on us!" or "Help us"? Let's try it. *(The children look sad and cry out for help.)* Great! The lepers were very sad and sick people.

Jesus heard their cries and wanted to help so he said, "Go and show yourselves to the priests." *(Say to the volunteer who is Jesus:)* "Would you please raise your arm and point over there to where the priests are, like Jesus did, and tell the lepers to "Go!" *(Child points in the direction you indicate and says "Go!")* Thank you!

Then, as the ten lepers obeyed Jesus and started walking away *(as you start this sentence, begin helping the children peel off their white spots)*, they looked at their arms and hands and saw that their leprosy had disappeared. They were healed! Jesus had made them all better! Children *(gesture to the "lepers")*, please show us with your faces and motions how happy the lepers must have felt when they knew they were well. *(Smiles, jumping up and down, saying, "Yeah, I'm well!", other responses.)* Yes, they were very happy.

Now, the rest of the people *(motion to the observer group)* weren't afraid of them anymore and wanted to be near them. Children, you can come back over here by this group *(the observer group joins the "lepers" group)* and please show us happy faces now instead of afraid faces. Now you even dare touch their arms or shake their hands. *(Responses.)*

That story turned out really well. Jesus made ten sick people well. Jesus healed them, and he deserved thanks. Let's thank Jesus for all the times he has healed us. *(Ask child who is Jesus to come forward.)* Let's say all together, "Thank you, Jesus!" Here we go. *(Children say the words.)*

And thank you, children, for acting out this story from the Bible. You helped us all remember that Jesus heals us and helps us in many ways, and we can say thank you. **–J.B.S.**

OCT. 18, 1998   OCT. 21, 2001   OCT. 17, 2004

The Gospel: Luke 18:1-8
Focus: Jesus encourages us to talk to God always, any time, anywhere, and about anything.
Experience: Through discussion and listing examples, the children learn that prayer is talking to God and can be done at any time.
Preparation: Gather pictures from magazines to illustrate the different times, places, and subjects that are involved in prayer (they illustrate the *when, where,* and *what* parts of the sermon.)

Pray Always!

(Greet the children.) Praying is talking to God. In our Bible reading today, Jesus says that we can always talk to God. Always means any time we want to talk to God we can. Let's think about that.

When are some times you and I talk to God? *(Bedtime, mealtime, other responses.)* We have thought of a lot of times we can talk to God. We can pray in the morning, before we eat, after we eat, in the afternoon, at suppertime and bedtime *(use magazine pictures of those times if you have them).* When you think of it, we can talk to God, or pray, any time. It could be at midnight or lunchtime.

We can also talk to God no matter *where* we are. Some moms and dads have told me that they talk to God while they are driving to work in their cars or riding on a bus. That's a quiet time when they can pray. You and I could do that, too. Where are some other places you and I can pray? *(Responses.)* That's a good list of places. We really can talk to God anywhere. It can be in our houses, outside, in our church, in our cars, on the bus, in school, in a hospital—no matter where we are God will hear what we are saying. You could be on top of a mountain or in a deep cave underground *(use magazine pictures if you have them)* and God would hear your prayer.

Now let's think about *what* we can talk to God about. We can talk about *anything* we are thinking about or care about! We can tell God when we are sad. We can ask God to help us at school. What are some other things we can talk to God about? *(When we're scared or worried, if someone is sick, when something nice happens, other responses.)* Thank you. There are a lot of things to talk to God about. We can talk to God about happy times or ask God to help a friend get well. We can ask God to bless our families. We can tell God "thank you" for making this beautiful world *(use magazine pictures if you have them).*

Jesus tells us that we can always talk to God. Always means at any time of the day, no matter where we are. We can also talk to God about anything we want to. God will always listen to us. That's good news. God loves us so much that God will always hear our prayers.

Let's talk to God right now. Please close your eyes and fold your hands and we will pray. Dear God, thank you for listening to us always. Help us to talk to you at many times and in many places about many things. Amen.
–J.B.S.

Sunday between October 23-29 inclusive, Proper 25

OCT. 25, 1998   OCT. 28, 2001   OCT. 24, 2004

The Gospel: Luke 18:9-14

Focus: Jesus calls us to pray to God, admitting that we are not perfect and that we need God's forgiveness and help.

Experience: Use a drawing of a girl named "Perfect Polly" to introduce the idea of perfection and illustrate that it is impossible to be perfect. Then talk with the children about our mistakes and that we can tell God about them.

Preparation: Make a drawing on tagboard or large sheet of paper of "Perfect Polly." (This can be as uncomplicated as a stick figure or rough drawing.) Print around the drawing descriptions of perfect behavior: "I never hit." "I never get grumpy." "I never yell or get mad."

We Need You

(Greet the children.) In the Bible Jesus tells us about a man who prayed a very short prayer. Listen to the man's prayer: "God, be merciful to me, a sinner!" Jesus tells us that this is a good prayer to pray. It is good because the man says that he is not perfect. He is saying that he makes mistakes and needs God's help. Jesus tells us about this man because Jesus wants you and me to think about how we are like him. We make mistakes and we need God's help, too.

I brought along a picture that I drew *(hold up "Perfect Polly")*. I call this person "Perfect Polly." She never makes mistakes. She always eats all her vegetables. She never hits her brother or sister. She never yells. She never gets mad at her parents or her friends.

"Perfect Polly" is *not* much like me and I'll bet she is not exactly like you either. You and I make mistakes. I remember that when I was your age I didn't always clean my room and make my bed. And even now, when I'm much older, I can still get grumpy with other people. Maybe you can think of some things like that that you do or don't do, too. What are some of them? *(Responses.)*

I made a drawing of "Perfect Polly" because that is all she really is. She's a drawing, she's just pretend *(fold up the drawing and discard it)*. No one is perfect like her. We all make mistakes. Sometimes we fight *(make a fist)*. Sometimes we won't share *(fold arms across your chest)* and we get mad *(make a grumpy face)*. Little people and big people *(gesture toward entire congregation)* do these things.

Jesus knows that you and I make mistakes. We don't have to pretend that we are perfect. Jesus says that we can tell God about it and ask for God's help. God loves you and me so much that God will forgive and help us.

We can pray prayers like these: Dear God, I hit my sister. I am sorry. Please help us not to fight. Amen. *Or:* Dear God, I wouldn't share my toys today. I'm sorry. Please help me to share with other people. Amen.

Those prayers are like the prayer the man in our Bible story prayed when he said, "God, be merciful to me, a sinner!" When we pray prayers like this God promises to listen and to help us.

Let's pray now. Please close your eyes and fold your hands. Dear God, we make mistakes and we need your love and help and forgiveness. Amen.
–J.B.S.

Sunday between October 30—November 5 inclusive, Proper 26

The Gospel: Luke 19:1-10
Focus: When we find out how much Jesus loves us, we change and become more loving and generous.
Experience: By acting out the story of Zacchaeus, the children see the difference Jesus' friendship can make in their lives.
Preparation: Practice the story.

When You Have
Two Strikes against You

(Greet the children.) Today we will think about what you can do when you have two strikes against you. Does anybody know what that means? *(Responses.)* It comes from baseball. What if you were up to bat, and two times the ball was pitched to you, and you swung at it and missed both times. You would have two strikes against you. And if you got three strikes, you would be out.

So when we say you have two strikes against you, we mean that things are not going your way, and if one more thing goes wrong, it will be a bad time for you.

Now let's pretend. This story is from the Bible. You are someone who lives in the same country as Jesus did. Other people say you have two strikes against you, not in baseball but in your life. But today might be your lucky day because you heard that Jesus is coming to town, right down the main street this morning, and you really want to meet him. You get up extra early and walk down to the main street two hours early to be sure to get a good spot to see Jesus. Let's pretend to be walking *(step in place.)*

But guess what, many people are already here, and some have been here all night. The place is packed. For sure you won't be able to see Jesus! Let's all say, "Oh, no!" *(You all say, "Oh, no!" and put one hand to your foreheads.)*

Earlier I said you have two strikes against you. Do you know what two things are problems for you? *(No.)* I will tell you. One is that you are a person who is very short, so you can't see over other people's heads in this crowd. The other is that nobody likes you because you have been cheating. So nobody will let you squeeze in beside them or in front of them to see Jesus.

What can you do about strike one, being short? What can you do so you can see Jesus? *(Prompt as needed. Climb on a roof. Get a stepladder. Climb a tree.)* Great! Let's say you climb a tree. Let's pretend we're climbing *(everyone reaches one hand above the other as though climbing).* And sure enough, you see Jesus and he sees you! *(All wave at Jesus.)* He asks if he can come to your house today. What will you answer? Let's all say, "Yes! Just follow me." *(The children all say "Yes! Just follow me.")* So we have taken care of strike one about being so short.

Now, what about strike two? How can you get people to like you again? *(Stop cheating. Promise not to do it again. Apologize.)* Will those things work? Maybe. Maybe not. Maybe not right away. Even if you do give back what you have stolen, some people will still not trust you, but some might. At least you would feel good in your heart that you did the right thing.

The person we have been pretending to be is Zacchaeus. He was a short man and nobody liked him because he was a tax collector who cheated people when they paid him their taxes. He took more money than he should have.

When Jesus came to his house, Zacchaeus listened to Jesus and changed from being a cheater into being a helper. He said he wasn't going to cheat any more. He was going to give half of his money to the poor, and he was going to pay everybody back four times what he had cheated them. He was going to become friendly, loving, and generous.

Not everybody became his friend right away. But he made one friend right away. Do you know who that was? *(Jesus.)* Yes, it was Jesus. Jesus is the most important friend anyone can have, and he wants to be your friend, too.

Let's pray. Jesus, thank you for becoming Zacchaeus's friend. Thank you for being my friend. Help me to remember how to be a good friend by being generous and not cheating. Amen. **–W.C.Y.**

Sunday between November 6-12 inclusive, Proper 27

NOV. 8, 1998   NOV. 11, 2001   NOV. 7, 2004

The Gospel: Luke 20:27-38

Focus: Our experience of the church begins with our immediate congregation but grows to include people all over the earth and those who have died and gone before us.

Experience: The children will begin by talking about what a family is and then look at the many circles that make up the church family.

Preparation: Make a chart with concentric circles on newsprint or tagboard, putting these words in the circles, moving from the center outward: family, church family, church family around the world, church family that lasts forever.

Who's Our Family?

(Greet the children.) Boys and girls, let's talk about family. What's a family? *(Responses. Parents and kids. Everyone who lives together. My family has a cat, too. All the animals in the world. Grandma and grandpa are in our family, too.)*

OK. Let's talk about who is in our family. All the people who live in our home are our family. And that would include parents and kids, and it might include grandparents or other relatives, too. We also consider relatives who do not live with us to be part of the family. When they all get together, we call that a family reunion. This might include grandparents, aunts, uncles, cousins, and might include a mother and a father for some of us whose parents are divorced.

What about somebody who lives with our family but wasn't born to our family, like an exchange student? We would probably tell this person when she or he came to live with us that she or was part of the family. If someone came and stayed a week we would treat them as family, too. Most of us probably would say to that person, "While you are with us, you are family. Make yourself at home." Sometimes we even refer to people who are our friends as being "just like a member of the family." Sometimes teenagers will say that a friend's mother is "my other mother" or a neighbor "my second father." So a family can be quite big, can't it? *(Yes.)*

Maybe you have heard someone call the people at church our church family. *(Bring out your chart.)* This chart shows our own family at the center, and our church family next. Who belongs to our church family? *(Everybody. Anybody who wants to.)* Anybody **can** belong to the church family, and in fact we are always inviting other people to become members of our church family. We want our church family to be big!

Our church family goes much farther than our church here in *(name your city or area)*. It stretches over the whole earth. *(Point to the next concentric circle on your chart.)* What kinds of people are in the world-wide church? *(People from all over the world. All races, all ages, people from all countries.)* This would include people who are hungry in Ethiopia and people who are picking bananas in El Salvador and Costa Rica, and people who make our shoes in Taiwan, and people in many other places, too.

And do you know what else? Our church family even includes people who are not alive on the earth any more. It says right here in the Bible that the people who have died, like Moses and Abraham are still alive. Some day we will be just like them, one big family sharing eternal life with God. *(Point out the last concentric circle, the church family that lasts forever.)*

But for now we need to work on living like one big family on earth. We can love and be kind to people in our own families, to those in our church right here, and to others farther away.

Let's pray. Dear God, thank you for giving us such a big family to love and enjoy. Help us to be willing to work together and find ways to help each other. Amen. **–W.C.Y.**

The Gospel: Luke 21:5-19

Focus: By reminding ourselves of God's love and protection, we find inner strength to deal with bad things that happen.

Experience: The children will think about bad things that can happen and what they can do to comfort themselves.

Preparation: Bring enough small stones so that each child can have one. If you can get polished stones, do so. *Option:* For regular stones, paint a cross on each one.

Comfort in Bad Times

(*Greet the children.*) Today I want to talk with you about a some sayings people use. Here's one: "Sticks and stones may break my bones, but names will never hurt me." Have you ever heard anyone say that? (*Yes. No. Not sure.*) When I say that, I'm saying that if people hit me with sticks and throw stones at me, I may get hurt, but if they call me bad names, I won't get hurt. But I'm not sure that's true. I don't want them to call me names. Do you like it when people call you names? (*No.*) Do you bleed or get your bones broken if someone calls you a bad name? (*No.*) But it still hurts, doesn't it? Why does it hurt, and where? (*Responses. It means they don't like me. Inside, in my heart, I feel bad.*)

Bad things do happen to us sometimes, don't they? We know we can pray to God and that God is always with us, even during bad times. It's also a good thing we have moms and dads who will listen and help us, and friends and teachers and other good people, too.

When bad things happen to us, we can say some other sayings to ourselves that might help us feel better. I will say each one first, then you say it after me: "God is always with me." (*The children repeat.*) "Jesus loves me, this I know." (*The children repeat.*) That one is from a song we often sing, isn't it? Here's one more: "God is my rock." * (*The children repeat.*) That one means that God is strong and protects us. Saying any of these sayings to ourselves is like saying a prayer, isn't it?

Let's say all three again: "God is always with me." "Jesus loves me, this

---

*This saying is a paraphraswe of Psalm 62:2.

I know." "God is my rock." *(The children repeat them after you.)*

I have something for you that fits with that last saying that God is my rock. I brought along some small stones. Each of you can have one to put in your pocket or hold in your hand. When you are worried about bad things that are happening, you can hold the stone and say, "God is my rock."

(Distribute the stones.) After each of you has a stone, I want you to hold it in your hand during our prayer. Let's pray. God, you are as strong as a rock. You protect us. We are never alone and we can always pray to you. Thank you for loving us. Amen. **–W.C.Y.**

The Gospel: Luke 23:33-43

Focus: We all need forgiveness.

Experience: The children will think about what they wish they hadn't done, listen to the leader give some examples, and talk about ways to get rid of bad things they have done. Only forgiveness can remove them.

Preparation: Bring a sheet of paper attached to a writing board, a marker or crayon, an eraser, and a wastebasket. Ask someone to play the role of a forgiving friend. Give him or her a copy of this sermon.

Forgiveness Gives Us a New Start

(Greet the children.) Boys and girls, today we're going to talk about forgiveness. If you accidentally broke a friend's toy or lost it, how would it feel if your friend said he or she would forgive you? (Responses. Good, relieved.) What does it mean to forgive? (Possible responses:. Not to be mad at that person anymore, to let go of bad feelings, to love people no matter what they did.) Forgiving is a good thing to do, isn't it? Then people can be friends again. Learning about forgiveness is very important.

When Jesus was on the cross, the first word that he thought to say was "forgive." He said, "Father, forgive them; for they do not know what they are doing." We learn a lot about forgiveness from Jesus. He seemed to be saying to all those people who were mean to him, "I forgive you." He forgave them, and he forgives us when we do wrong things, too.

Let's think about some things you have done that you wish you hadn't done. Can anyone think of something? (Do not press for responses or suggest responses if the children are reluctant.) Since you wish you hadn't done them, maybe you are not too eager to tell me with everybody listening to us. So let me make a list of some things that I have done that I wish I hadn't done.

(Give your own examples throughout this section.) I once hit a kid on the head with a baseball bat while taking some practice swings, and he needed stitches. It was an accident, but I felt bad. I am going to write that down. (Write "hit with a bat" or your example.) I once moved my brother's bike to a friend's house two blocks away and he thought someone stole it. I meant it to be a joke. *(Write "bad joke—moved bike" or your example. Keep on until you have three or four examples.)*

Once I did those things, I couldn't forget them. How do you think I felt about all these things? *(Bad. Worried. Afraid. Guilty.)* Yes, especially guilty. I could try hiding what I did *(put list under you and sit on it or put it in your pocket)*, but other people probably could still tell I was hiding something. I could try erasing what I did *(use an eraser on your paper)*, but I still remember them. I could try forgetting them, like throwing away this piece of paper, but I'm still afraid and guilty. *(Throw paper in wastebasket.)* I really have a problem, don't I?

(Enter a visitor who picks the list out of the wastebasket.)

VISITOR: (Your name), what's on this paper you threw away?

YOU: Oh, it's nothing.

VISITOR: I just read it. It seems to be a list of bad things you have done. You might feel bad thinking about all this, but, *(your name)*, remember that God loves you and forgives you. If there is anybody on this list that you still need to apologize to, I'll be glad to go with you when you do it. Then you and I can go to a ball game *(or some other activity)* and forget about this list.

YOU: Thank you. You're a good friend to remind me that I am forgiven. *(To the children:)* And I will remind each of you that God loves and forgives you, too. That is really good news.

Let's pray. God, thank you for loving us and forgiving us when we do what we wish we hadn't. Remind us to forgive others and help us to apologize when we need to. Amen. **–W.C.Y.**

The Gospel: John 8:31-36
Focus: Jesus sets us free; we are forgiven.
Experience: The children will first think about what it's like to be a slave and then hear about the reformer Martin Luther, who discovered he was forgiven because of Jesus.
Preparation: Bring a Bible and a picture of Martin Luther.

Slavery or Freedom

(Greet the children.) Sometimes in stories or movies we hear about people called slaves. Do you know what a slave is? *(Responses. Somebody owned by someone else. Someone who works hard but doesn't get any money. A person who isn't free.)*

We don't allow slaves in our country anymore, but sometimes we use the word when we think we're working too hard. My mother used to say, "I'm not your slave" when we kids kept asking her to do all kinds of things for us.

Think about how it would feel to be a real slave. You'd work hard for no money and get yelled at and hit. Let's pretend you are shoveling dirt and stones, and that you are getting so tired. *(You and the children pretend to shovel, wipe your foreheads.)* Maybe you'd have to sleep on a hard mat on the floor and barely get enough to eat. Then what if a kind person came and set you free. You wouldn't be a slave anymore! You could throw your shovels away. *(Pretend to throw them.)* How would you feel? *(Responses. Happy, feel great, jump up and down, can hardly believe it, thankful to the one who freed me.)*

Today is Reformation Sunday. That's a long word, isn't it? You'll learn more about it when you get older. It's the day we remember a man named Martin Luther, born in Germany, and all the good things he did. This is not Martin Luther King Jr., who was from the United States; he came much later and he was named for Martin Luther. *(Show picture of Martin Luther if you have one.)*

Poor Martin Luther! He felt like a slave to sin, a slave to the bad things he kept doing. He wanted to be good, but knew he was doing so many things wrong. He was so sad and was sure God hated him. Then one wonderful day he was reading the Bible *(hold up Bible)* and found out that Jesus forgave him his sins and he was free of them! God loved him!

Remember how we said it would feel if you were a slave and someone set you free? *(Review what they said, happy, thankful, etc.)* That's how Martin Luther felt.

From then on, Martin Luther talked to people, preached sermons, and wrote books about how much God loves us. Because of what Jesus did, we are forgiven and *free*! Jesus said that without him, we are like slaves. We aren't free. But Jesus loves us very much and forgives us these bad things we do, so now we are free!

So let's answer yes or no to these questions. First, are you a slave? *(No! Repeat question and answer, perhaps have the congregation join in.)* Next, because of Jesus, are you free? *(Yes! Repeat as with the first question.)*

Let's pray. God, we are so happy that we are not slaves. Thank you for sending Jesus so that we are free! We are loved and forgiven. Help us to tell others this good news. Amen. **–W.C.Y.**

All Saints' Sunday

The Gospel: Luke 6:20-31

Focus: One aspect of All Saints' Day is that we all are saints in God's eyes because we are forgiven through Jesus. Another aspect, from the church's tradition, is that exemplary Christians have been called saints.

Experience: By talking about what people called saints did to earn that title and looking at a news story about a saintly person today, the children will realize that they, too, can do what Jesus wants them to do.

Preparation: Bring a book on saints from the juvenile section of the public library. Also, cut from newspaper some example of a modern day saint or use the story described below. Prepare to sing or have sung the third verse of "I Sing a Song of the Saints of God" or another song about saints, such as "For All the Saints" (Lutheran Book of Worship, 174).

The Saints of God

(Greet the children.) Girls and boys, today is All Saints' Day. Do you know the names of people who have been called saints—Saint Joan, or Saint somebody? *(Responses will vary. Examples: St. George who killed the dragon. St. Paul's Church. St. Francis. Adapt your comments to fit their responses.)* Yes, there is St. George who slew the dragon, and there is St. Francis who preached to the animals. Some churches are named for saints. The church down the street *(adapt to your situation)* is named for St. Paul, the great missionary of the Bible. There is also St. Joan of Arc who led her people into battle against the English, and there is St. Patrick, the missionary to the Irish. We remember him each year on St. Patrick's Day, March 17.

Those saints were people who tried to do what Jesus taught. They were very loving—loving everybody, even their enemies. Some saints got into trouble. They saw what needed to be done and made good changes, but their enemies didn't like what they did.

It sounds like the saints are all dead, but they aren't. Just as the saints that we have talked about were once alive, so today there are people who are saints because they try to do what Jesus wants, and they show love and do good no matter what the danger. I have a picture here of a man that I cut out of the newspaper *(adapt to your situation)*. This man was walking by a house last week when he heard children screaming. Seeing that the house was on fire, he went to a window, broke it, and helped get the children out. I'd say he was a saint. What do you think? *(Yes.)* Who else might be called a saint? (*Responses. Be prepared to use your own examples.*)

The Bible calls all who follow Jesus saints. All of us who are forgiven by Jesus can be called saints. That means you are a saint (*point to a child*) and you and you (*point to all of them*), and so am I, and so are all those people (*point to the congregation*). So that is one meaning of the word saint.

Another meaning is that saints are very holy or good people. They do what Jesus taught, making peace, helping the hungry or homeless, forgiving others, and showing love to everybody. God wants us to try to be like that, too.

There's a song I'd like to sing for you (*or have the choir or someone else sing for you*) that will serve as our prayer. Listen carefully to it.

They lived not only in ages past,
There are hundreds of thousands still;
The world is bright with the joyous saints!
Who love to do Jesus' will.
You can meet them in school, on the street, in the store,
in church, by the sea, in the house next door:
For the saints of God can be rich or poor,
And I mean to be one, too. *

(*This may be sung by the leader, the choir, or congregation. Additional verses, typically 1 and 2, may be sung by the congregation as children return to their seats or leave the sanctuary.*)

–W.C.Y.

* "I Sing a Song of the Saints of God," *Rejoice in the Lord: A Hymn Companion to the Scriptures*, Erik Routley, ed. Grand Rapids: Wm. B. Eerdmans Publishing Co. 1985.

The Gospel: John 6:25-35

Focus: We are grateful for bread and for Jesus as the bread of life.

Experience: The children will name and hold symbols of ingredients and objects needed to make bread, and they will create a litany of thanksgiving for bread.

Preparation: Gather a number of items that are needed for making bread. Essential are flour, water, yeast, oil or shortening, salt, bowl, spoon, and bread pan. You could also bring wheat (or picture of wheat), soil, change purse with money in it, recipe, measuring cup, and small oven (or oven thermometer or matches). Bring a picture of Jesus or a cross. If you can, obtain the music for "Thank You, Thank You" by Avery and Marsh.

The Bread of Life

(Greet the children.) Girls and boys, when Jesus said "I am the bread of life," he reminded us that bread is very important. When somebody is so poor that they can't afford much food, they will buy or bake or beg for bread, because it is filling, nourishing, and cheap to make. Sometimes we talk about breaking bread together, and by that we mean let's eat together. Somebody might come up to you on the street and say, "I need some bread." That means, "I need money to buy food with." So, you see, bread is important to life.

Since bread is so important, I thought that we could say prayers of thanksgiving for bread as a way to thank God for everything that goes into making bread. I have brought many of the ingredients and other things that it takes to make bread. Could some of you help me hold things as we talk about them and write our prayer? (Yes.) Thank you.

First we need flour. Who would like to hold the flour? (Each time, hand items to children as you name them.) Next we need water, yeast, and oil (or shortening) for our bread. Could three of you hold them? And salt, we'll need a dash or two of that. Could you hold that? Now what do we need to mix all these things together? A bowl and a spoon. Two people can hold those. Now we need a bread pan to put the dough into. Can you hold that?

(If you have brought other items, also talk about them as follows.) Flour comes from wheat, so can somebody please hold this shaft of wheat (or wheat kernels or picture of wheat)? Wheat grows in soil, so can somebody hold this can *(or bag)* of soil, and any worms that may be in it! Without money to buy the ingredients with, we wouldn't be able to make bread, so will somebody hold the change purse? *(Mention recipe, measuring cup, and items other than the oven or matches that you have brought.)*

Once we have all the ingredients and pretend we have mixed them, is it bread yet? Of course not! Now we're going to need a fire or an oven to bake the bread. Can someone hold the matches to light a fire *(or the small oven or oven thermometer)?*

Now let's pretend our bread is baked and it is time to eat the bread. Those of you who aren't holding things, please hold hands with each other.

At every meal, there is somebody with us, somebody we can't see, an unseen guest. His name is Jesus. He calls himself the bread of life. Will one of you please hold this picture of Jesus *(or cross)* so that we can all see it? Thanks.

Now we are ready for our prayers. We need to learn a line to say after each of our prayers, so I am going to teach it to you. There are two words that we repeat three times, and one word we repeat three times, and one word we add at the end of the line. * * *(If you don't have the songbook, speak the words rather than sing them.)*

"Thank you, thank you, thank you, Lord." Let's practice it.

Our prayers go like this. I am going to say "We thank you, God, for . . ." and name something. When I point to you, you hold up real high your ingredient and say what it is, and then we will all sing *(or say)* our response and the congregation can join us. OK, let's begin.

> We thank you, God, for *(flour).*
> Thank you, thank you, thank you, Lord.
>
> *(Continue the litany for all the items. You could add an ending prayer, such as "We thank you, God, for all you give us.)*
>
> Thank you all for doing so well. Happy Thanksgiving!

–W.C.Y.